A TRENCHERMAN'S GU[...]
TO THE
EASTERN C[...]

COMPILED AND EDITED BY: JA[...]

C O N T E N T

Restaurants:

Inns & Pubs:

NO PAYMENT HAS BEEN ACCEPTED
FOR ENTRY TO THIS GUIDE

Published by:-
Bracken Publishing, Cromer, Norfolk
ISBN: 1 871614 27 9
Printed by Broadgate Printers, Aylsham, Norfolk
November 1997

ADNAMS

DRAUGHT BROADSIDE
Has the generous character of
the famous Broadside bottled beer.
Well rounded, slightly bitter sweet.
An important addition to our range.

"From Suffolk's Oldest Brewery, Britain's Finest Beer"
ADNAMS & CO. PLC.
SOLE BAY BREWERY, SOUTHWOLD, SUFFOLK **IP18 6JW**
TEL : 01502 727200 FAX:01502 727201

▲▼▲

RESTAURANTS

▲▼▲

IMPORTANT

Please note:-

1. Dishes listed are examples only. Menus change frequently, so they will not necessarily be available at all times.

2. Prices, where quoted, may change during the currency of this guide. Average a la carte prices are based on a three course meal without wine, unless otherwise stated.

3. Open hours refer to meals only, up until last orders are taken, unless otherwise stated.

4. Every effort is made to ensure accuracy, but inevitably circumstances alter and errors and omissions may occur. Therefore the publisher cannot accept liability for any consequences arising therefrom.

5. This is a selection: it is not claimed that all the best establishments in the region are featured.

THIS GUIDE IS PRODUCED QUITE INDEPENDENTLY, AND
HAS NO CONNECTION WITH ANY COMPANY
OR PUBLICATION OF A SIMILAR NAME.

NO PAYMENT HAS BEEN ACCEPTED
FOR ENTRY TO THIS GUIDE

EDELWEISS SWISS RESTAURANT
1613 London Road, Leigh-on-Sea. Tel: (01702) 711517

Hours: 7 to 10pm, Mon. - Sat; private lunches by arrangement.
Credit cards: Mastercard, Visa, Amex.
Price guide: a la carte £26 - 28 (incl. drinks); 'Schnitzel' menu £12
(Mon - Thurs only).

Examples from menus (specials vary daily): *graubundner fleisch (air-cured beef served on wooden plate with black bread); coquilles d'homard "William Tell" (lobster meat served on shredded apple, lettuce with horseradish mayonnaise, boiled egg); Tournedo Heligoland (fillet steak filled with lobster, roasted with tarragon, in white wine cream sauce); Basler lummelbraten (fillet steak larded with pork fat, roasted & sliced with kidney, served with roast potatoes, celery & cream sauce); vegetarian dishes; flambes; fondues. Sweets & savouries.*

From land-locked mountainous Switzerland to the flat Essex coast - the contrast could hardly be starker, but chef patron Herbert Staudhammer has successfully established this outpost of his scenic home country here over the past 18 years (though not at Swiss prices!). He began in Zurich, garnering further experience from Germany, Paris and at the German Food Centre in Knightsbridge. These influences are brough to bear on his mouthwatering Franco-Germanic menus (only freshest ingredients), though he will be pleased to meet special 'exotic' requests if given sufficient notice - steak & kidney pudding and spotted dick are past examples! The cosy restaurant seats just 40, but there's only one sitting, so one may relax and maybe share a fondue, a most sociable way of eating, accompanied perhaps by one of 14 uncommon Swiss wines.

CAFÉ ROCOCO
34 - 36 Elm Road, Leigh-on-Sea. Tel: (01702) 711141 Fax: (01702) 713617

Hours: 12 to 3pm, 6 to 10pm Mon - Sat; 12 to 3pm Sun.
Credit cards: Mastercard, Visa, Amex, Diners, Switch, Delta, Electron, JCB.
Price guide: a la carte dinner £16, lunches from about £5.

Examples from menus (revised monthly): *eggs scrambled with butter & cream, in filo pastry case with dressed raspberry salad; parisienne of three melons with exotic fruits & smoked salmon; spiced chicken & pineapple cocktail. Cajun grills; monkfish, crab & asparagus crepes; minced beef ragu topped with julienne of smoked ham; ricotta cheese & broccoli cannelloni; many specials eg kangaroo kebabs, grilled fillet of snapper (in chardonnay, cream & grape sauce), wild mushroom & tarragon croquettes in sun-dried tomato sauce. Belgian apple tart with raspberry custard; dark chocolate mousse with creme anglais, laced with Grand Marnier; bread & banana pudding. Trad. Sun. roasts plus alternatives.*

'Eclectic' is perhaps a rather overworked word, but it is most apposite here. Every corner of the world appears to be represented on a menu that is decidedly different, and it's all down to the years spent by Paul Christian traversing the globe. With brother Bryan and chef Richard James, he has brought exciting ideas to this novel, stylish restaurant amongst the shops of Leigh town centre. First they had to completely refurbish the old building, and chose the Rococo mode of cool elegance and soft pastel colours. Opening in June 1994, they have built a loyal following, and continue to offer excellent value. Weddings and other private functions catered for. Outside catering service. Easy parking on street or nearby car park. Close to seafront gardens and promenade. Outside catering service

PARIS RESTAURANT
719 London Road, Westcliff-on-Sea. Tel. & Fax: (01702) 344077

Hours: 12 to 2pm, 7 to 10pm, except Sun evenings and all day Mons.
Credit cards: Mastercard, Visa, Switch, Delta.
Price guide: set price dinner £20.95 & £24.95 (2 & 3 courses); set
price lunch £13.95 & £15.95 (2 & 3 courses); with coffee & petits fours.
Sample menus on request.

Examples from seasonal menus (revised daily): *prawn, bean & truffle vinaigrette; nicoise salad with fresh tuna; squid with a honey & chilli dressing. John Dory, spring onion & crayfish; oriental duck; sea bass in pastry, chive sauce & asparagus (pictured); seafood platter for 2,(24 hrs notice); beef fillet with rich red wine sauce; lamb with celeriac & wild mushrooms. Triple raspberry delight; apple tart with blackberry ice cream; peaches in a champagne soup. Trad. Sun. roasts, vegetarian platter. Selection of cheeses from Paris markets.*

Don't be misled: this is not a French restaurant, but it does share its name with proprietor Wayne Hawkins' daughter. There is French influence, of course, but Wayne and his team draw on the world's cuisine to develop their own unique style. Customers, who often travel from afar, obviously like it, for business continues to flourish after seven years in the unlikely setting of suburban Southend. The decor is stylish, slick but comfortable, the atmosphere sophisticated but welcoming. Wayne also operates a highly profesional outside catering service (with staff if required). Easy street parking in the evenings. Full programme of special events (incl. Ladies' Night) - ask to go on the mailing list.

ALVARO'S
32 St. Helen's Road, Westcliff-on-Sea. Tel: (01702) 335840

Hours: 12 to 2pm Tues-Fri, 7 to 10:30pm Tues-Sun (11pm Fri & Sat).
Credit cards: Mastercard, Visa, Switch.
Price guide: a la carte from £22.

Examples from menus (revised periodically): *langoustines sautéed in spicy Portuguese piri-piri butter; salted cod (with onion, potato, black olives & egg). Portuguese fish casserole; fillets of sole in light egg batter (pan-fried with banana, Madeira style), beef Alvaro's (large sirloin pan fried in butter with onions, mushrooms, artichokes, & wine, finished with brandy & cream); roast half duckling in port wine sauce; speciality espetadas. Crepes & flambes.*

"Nao faz mal" (it doesn't matter) could be described as Portugal's motto, but this laid-back philosophy doesn't extend to the kitchen. Good food is taken very seriously, and there are no better exponents than Alvaro ('Freddy') Rodrigues and brother Jose (who cooks); together they have re-created a little corner of their beautiful country here over the past twenty-something years. Immaculate cleanliness, attentive but unobtrusive service, atmosphere and decor are all authentically Portuguese, with the theme of carved and painted cockerels, a legendary national symbol. Naturally seafood is always to the fore, though steaks, pork, poultry etc, are well featured, and you will find a very fine range of Portuguese wines and old ports - you may also like to try one of the excellent Portuguese beers. Rated highly by both national guides and local people, Alvaro's is just off the main shopping street; from the A127 or A13 take the first left by the lights at Victoria Station onto Hamlet Court Road, then third left - check when you book.

HOTEL RENOUF
Bradley Way, Rochford. Tel: (01702) 544393 Fax: (01702) 549563

Hours: 12 to 1:45pm, 7 to 9:45pm daily except Sat lunch;
(residents only Sun evenings).
Credit cards: Mastercard, Visa, Diners, Amex, Switch, Delta.
Price guide: a la carte £25, table d'hote £15.50 & £17.50 (2 & 3 courses).
Accommodation: 7 sngls (from £49.50), 14 dbls/twins (from £69.50), 1 executive
(from £84.50), 2 suites (from £89.50); all en-suite, satellite TV, phone,
hair dryer, tea & coff; suites have spa bath, bath robes,
trouser press and mini bar.

Examples from menus (a la carte revised seasonally, table d'hote weekly): *smokey venison with beetroot sauce; prawn & smoked salmon strudel; watercress & lime soup. Pressed duck Roenaise (speciality); crab Derek (in wine sauce with smoked halibut, coriander & cheese); bass in pastry with lobster & sorrel sauce; sliced fillet of lamb with seared vegetables & provencal sauce; chicken stuffed with avocado, with sage & lemon sauce; vegetable pancakes with tomato Neopolitan sauce. Home-made sweets. Trad. Sun roasts plus alternatives £12.50 & £17.50 (2 & 3 courses).*

"Seeing is deceiving; it's eating that's believing." Framed on a wall near the entrance, this bon mot has served Derek Renouf well in his 40 years as a a head chef, the last 11 here at his own luxury hotel. Son Melvin is taking up the reins, and it's quite a legacy: the RAC rates this as one of the top 200 establishments in the country, an enthusiasm consistently shared by every other guide of note, and by guests, of course. Seven chefs mean that a huge choice does not compromise standards. Try the 'Discovery' menu, described as "a search for new and tantalizing tastes from all parts of the world". Bedrooms are spacious and very well appointed, public rooms also - look for the reproduction Bayeux Tapestry (Renoufs came with The Conqueror) and collection of historic cricket bats. Function rooms overlook lovely garden and pond.

THE CONTENTED SOLE
80 High Street, Burnham-on-Crouch. Tel: (01621) 782139

Hours: 12 to 2pm Tues - Sun; 7 to 9:30pm Tues - Sat.
Credit cards: Mastercard, Visa, Switch, Delta.
Price guide: a la carte £27, table d'hote (lunch & dinner) £10.95 & £12.95;
Sun. lunch £10.95 - £12.95.

Examples from menus (table d'hote revised monthly, a la carte seasonally): *potted prawns & salmon set in Gewurtzraminer jelly, surrounded by slices of king scallops marinated with lime, green peppercorns & capers; filo pastry basket filled with mixed leaf salad tossed in cider vinaigrette topped with slices of Indian spiced chicken. Roasted local sea bass stuffed with spring onions & ginger, with light soy sauce dressing; pan-fried slices of pork with prune & pear farce with stock sauce; specials eg scallops & bacon, lobster dishes, game in season. Crispy apple fritters with apricot sauce & cream; light white Belgian chocolate mousse on dark chocolate sponge with passion fruit coulis. Trad. Sun. roasts plus alternatives.*

In the hands of the Walton family since 1965, this has long been recognised as one of the county's top restaurants, if also (in the past) one of the most formal and expensive. But a new generation has meant a new approach: Simon and Tamar Walton, while maintaining the high standards which have kept a place in most of the prestigious national guides, have dropped the dress code and prices - the table d'hote especially represents extremely good value - but have greatly increased portions. Chef Tim Morris (ex Cliveden and Loch Torridon) says nouvelle cuisine is well and truly passé. The two dining rooms and reception area have also undergone a sumptuous facelift: light pastel colours, Japanese oak panelling, fine art (for sale - the Waltons also run 'Sole Art'). Ask about the programme of events, such as wine tasting, golf days, seafood week, lobster lunches etc.

BARLEYLANDS RESTAURANT
Barleylands Road, Billericay. Tel: (01268) 289963

Hours: 10:30am to 4pm daily; 7 to 9:30pm Tues - Sat.
Credit cards: Mastercard, Visa, Diners, Switch, Delta.
Price guide: a la carte £25, table d'hote (evening) £15.95, lunch £7.50-£8 & £10
(2 & 3 courses); Wed. evenings "PAY WHAT YOU THINK"
(not incl. wine).

Examples from dinner menus (revised monthly): *Madame Milbert's rabbit terrine; fresh salmon rosti with wild mushrooms; three-cheese strudel on julienne of celery & leek. Fresh fish daily eg halibut in whole grain mustard sauce; steak, Guinness & fresh oyster pie; glazed duck breast with apricots marinated in white rum. Toffee pie with caramelised banana; white & dark chocolate torte; baked Alaska tartlet.* Lunch: *home-made pies; braised liver & onion with bacon; chilli; salads; pasta dishes; sandwiches; Trad. Sun. roasts plus alternatives (£11.50 for 3 courses). Cream teas, home-made scones & bread etc.*

Not so long ago any eating place attached to a tourist attraction conjured up images of concrete scones, stewed tea and cheap laminates. If ever there were a measure of how much things have improved, this superbly converted barn is it: not only a first-quality tearoom serving tasty home-made light lunches, but metamorphosing into a high class restaurant by evening. It's the achievement of young chef proprietor (since 1996) Darren Bennett, who has worked at Renouf's (qv) and Michelin-starred London restaurants. His brave and novel offer that Wednesday diners pay what they feel the meal was worth has not left him out of pocket. There's a great day out to be had at the adjacent Farm Museum & Visitors' Centre: steam engines, glass blowing, miniature railway, farm animals and implements, play area; but you could eschew all that for a restaurant worth visiting on its own merit. Outside catering, private dinner parties (staffed) and high class hampers are specialities.

THE DUKE OF YORK
Southend Road, Billericay (A 129) Tel: (01277) 651403

Hours: Restaurant 12 to 2pm, 7 to 10pm weekdays; Saturdays 7 to 10pm;
Sundays 12 to 2:30pm. Pub hours for bar food as above
plus Sat. 12 to 2:15pm. OPEN ALL DAY FOR DRINKS.
Credit cards: Mastercard, Visa, Diners, Amex.
Price guide: a la carte (also in French & German) £20 - £25; table d'hote £16;
bar meals from £3.85; Sunday lunch (roast £4.75). Booking advised.

Examples from menus: *courgettes provencal; smoked eel in garlic butter. Fillet of salmon in crab & mussel sauce; local trout Bretonne; strips of veal in tomato & cream sauce; supreme of chicken with bacon & cider sauce; strips of fillet steak in dill & coriander sauce; spinach & tomato roulade with hollandaise sauce; tandoori vegetables on bed of rice; grills; many daily specials. Crepes Suzettes; homemade sweets & gateaux. Trad. Sun. roasts.* Bar: *chicken Italienne; home-made pies; fresh skate; Cantonese prawns; fresh pasta dishes.*

Even though the menus are enormous, pride is taken in the freshness of all ingredients. Fish, for example, is delivered daily from the London markets, and some of the sweets and gateaux are made on the premises. Chef proprietor David White specialises in delicious sauces of all kinds, but will cook any dish to customer requirements - flexibility that is the stamp of a family-run business. Those who prefer their food without adornment have a wide choice of grilled meats and fish, and vegetarians have their own separate menu of at least 10 alternatives. Bar meals (except light snacks) may be taken in the restaurant. Over 120 wines from all over the world are listed with helpful descriptions, and staff are all well trained in the subject - hence the Routiers Corps d'Elite Award. An outstanding selection of malt whiskies would delight even the most discerning Scot! The antique cash register (in £. s. d.) will stir a little nostalgia.

LITTLE HAMMONDS
51 High Street, Ingatestone. Tel: (01277) 353194

Hours: 12 to 2:30pm, 6 to 11pm, 7 days per week (closed Bank Holidays).
Credit cards: Mastercard, Visa, Switch.
Price guide: a la carte £25.50 set price; table d'hote (Sun evening to Sat lunch)
£17.95 & £10 (lMon - Sat lunch, excl. Thurs, Fri & Sat evenings); Sun.
lunch £12.95; 'Magic Night' on Sun evenings - with magician
& pasta, 2 courses £5.95.

Examples from menus (revised quarterly, plus daily specials): *tartlet of smoked chicken & avocado with spicy peanut sauce; ravioli of Cornish crab on buttered leeks with Thai dressing. Little Hammond's vegetarian risotto; roasted cod with mussels & clams in saffron & tomato nage; breast of guinea fowl stuffed with wild mushrooms & parma ham. Florentine sablée; banana tartlet with butterscotch sauce; flambé desserts. Trad. Sun. roasts plus alternatives.*

NB: Little Hammond's Gold Card (cost £20) entitles holder to 10% discount for 6 months.

Proprietor Stuart Hammond acquired his expertise at various high class hotels and restaurants, and opened here in August 1987. The 'Little' refers to the cottage in which it is housed, which dates from 1558 and is apparently home to a number of ghosts, observed several times by Stuart and staff and the subject of a TV documentary. Undaunted, head chef Kevin Hannaford continues to offer a combination of the best new ideas in cooking, including his own creations, at amazing prices: £10 for a three-course meal is unbeatable value. The restaurant has excellent facilities for a special occasion: the 'Magic Cabaret' seats parties of 10, there is a no-smoking room seating 12 and another private room for 25. Stuart also runs a very professional outside catering service (tel. 352927) for all kinds of events. If the delicious aroma of fresh-baked bread wafts around you, don't look for the paranormal: Stuart's bakehouse is next door!

RUSSELLS RESTAURANT
Bell Street, Gt Baddow, nr Chelmsford. Tel: (01245) 478484 Fax: (01245) 472705

Hours: 12 to 2pm, 7 to 11pm
Tues - Sun; Mondays by
prior arrangement.
Credit cards: Mastercard, Visa,
Diners, Amex, Switch.
Price guide: a la carte £25
(5 courses), table d'hote
£16.95 (5 courses, not
Sat. evening), lunch
£10.95 (3 courses).

Examples from menu (table d'hote revised weekly, a la carte four-monthly): *pinwheel of chicken, spinach & pistachio nuts with white grape chutney; smoked salmon with tagliatelle, spring onions & toasted almonds bound with creamy vermouth sauce. Grilled noisettes of lamb on anna potato with blackcurrant & thyme sauce; breast of duck stufed with spinach & bacon wrapped in pastry lattice with rich port wine sauce; pepper-crusted monkfish on red pepper relish; leek & mustard crumble with creamy mushroom & tarragon sauce. Sweet pastry tart filled with raspberry & chocolate truffle; cheesecake roulade filled with forest fruit mousse on passion fruit coulis. Trad. Sun. roasts.*

For all the passing fads of recent years, the classical Anglo-French restaurant still occupies a prominent place. A skilled exponent, chef Mark Jeans prepares a menu of considerable diversity, among which are numbered many time-honoured favourites, plus vegetarian alternatives, and the last Thursday of every month is Gourmet Night. Guests are invited to say if they prefer food more plainly cooked. The building itself is decidedly English; built in 1372 as a barn, it has a high vaulted ceiling, a plethora of beams and exposed bricks, and a gallery overlooking the main dining area. Proprietors Barry and Juliet Watson have, due to a fire, regretfully had to restrict smoking to the lounge and bar. Excellent 82-strong international wine list. Disabled and conference facilites. Outside catering a speciality.

THE PUNCH BOWL
High Easter, nr Chelmsford. Tel: (01245) 231222

Hours: 7pm to 9:30pm Tues - Sat, plus Sun. lunch.
Credit cards: Mastercard, Visa, Amex, Switch.
Price guide: set price £28.90 Sats, £18.90 weekdays & lunch.

Examples from menus (revised seasonally): *Norfolk samphire; home-grown aspara-gus; moules mariniere. Filo pastry basket filled with smoked salmon, scrambled egg & cream; breast of duck with orange beurre blanc; individual beef Wellington; Cornish lobsters. Mrs Wright's butterscotch tart; champagne cocktails (speciality). Sunday lunch: roast sirloin of beef carved at the table.*

Consistency is surely a key to the long term success of any restaurant. Clearly the Punch Bowl possesses this quality in good measure, for it has remained amongst the county's best known and patronised for many years now, principally for good food on a diverse and interesting menu. Seven miles west of hectic Chelmsford, in a very different, more tranquil world, this Tudor building itself sets the stage: the 15th-century timbers and lovely solid willow floor are the backdrop for soft candlelight, fresh flowers and crisp linen. Many a memorable wedding reception has been held here, although in summer the marquee turns the lovely two-acre garden into a set for 'Camelot' - very romantic. From this same garden come the fresh flowers and herbs for the kitchen; freshness is paramount in all ingredients. Over 200 wines. Outside catering a speciality.

DUNMOW'S CHINA GARDEN RESTAURANT
27 (1st Floor) High Street, Gt Dunmow. Tel: (01371) 872845/875298

Hours: 12 to 2pm Mon - Fri; 5:30 to 11:30pm Mon - Wed, to midnight
Thurs & Fri; noon to midnight Sat; 12:30 to 3pm, 6 to 11:30pm Sun.
Credit cards: Mastercard, Visa, Diners, Amex.
Price guide: a la carte £15, set meals from £10.25.

Examples from menu: *deep-fried crab claws stuffed with mashed prawn & crab; stuffed green pepper in garlic & black bean sauce; Szechuan aromatic duck with pancakes. Peking-style sizzling sliced pork with spring onions in yellow bean sauce; deep-fried sweet & sour fish; Mongolian hot pot lamb; Szechuan-style kung po hot & sour chicken; lo han chai (vegetarian); shark's fin & vermicelli soup. Sunday lunch buffet £9.50 for adults, £5 for children under 12.*

Do not be put off by a rather unpromising frontage: this is no ordinary Chinese restaurant, but one which has rejoiced for many years in a widespread reputation for excellence. Opulent and roomy, its decor is as authentically Chinese as the cooking, and what a choice! The familiar Cantonese dishes are there amongst the 130 or so listed, but so too are Mongolian, Peking and Szechuan, considered superior. Knowledgeable waiters will explain the mysteries. A recent innovation is the Sunday lunch buffet - help yourself to an array of delights at modest cost. Not surprisingly it's very popular, but fortunately there are about 100 seats. Not on the menu are the exotic fish in an intriguing aquarium! Separate banqueting room for private functions. International wine list. Take away service. Large public car park to rear.

WHITEHALL HOTEL

Church End, Broxted, nr Stansted. Tel: (01279) 850603 Fax: (01279) 850385

Hours: 12 to 1:30pm, 7:30 to 10pm daily.
Credit cards: Mastercard, Visa, Diners, Amex.
Price guide: a la carte £34; table d'hote lunch £20 (3 courses).
Accommodation: 25 dbls/twins (£110 - £140, £80 as sngl); all en- suite,
TV, direct phone, hair dryer, trouser press; 2-day breaks
£130-160 per couple incl. dinner, b & b.

Examples from menus (revised monthly, lunch daily): *home-made game sausage with onions, chives & hot beetroot sauce; hot artichoke soufflé; pan-fried langoustines with trompett mushrooms & lobster cream sauce. Loin of wild hare with apple & celeriac rosti in light port jus; mille feuille of courgette & mushroom with spicy tomato sauce; fillet of sea bream with stir-fry vegetables & cashew nuts. Dark & white chocolate pyramid with milk chocolate mousse; hot mango & honey souffle; finest cheeses.*

Starting from scratch 12 years ago, the Keane family has placed this glorious Tudor mansion in the front rank of hotels and restaurants in the country, now part of the new Essex luxury hotel group Heritage Leisure. On the way it has earned numerous accolades and a regular place in all the main national guides. For all this, and the opulent surroundings, there is no hint of stuffiness; indeed, true to the family's Irish roots, informality is encouraged in a warm and friendly atmosphere. The restaurant is remarkable both for its extraordinary character - high vaulted ceiling and massive fireplace - and for the haute cuisine of chef Paula Keane. The six-course daily menu 'Surprise' is a speciality not to be missed. A spectacular barn suite makes a wonderful venue for a wedding reception and the lovely garden affords ample photo opportunities. Handy for Stansted Airport.

THE OLD HOOPS
15 King Street, Saffron Walden. Tel: (01799) 522813

Hours: 12 to 2:15pm, 7 to 9:30pm, Tues. - Sat.
Credit cards: Mastercard, Visa, Diners, Amex.
Price guide: a la carte dinner £20 - 25, lunch £10 - £15; set dinner
(Tues - Fri only) £11.95 & £12.95; lunch (all week) £6.95 & £7.95
respectively for 2 & 3 courses plus coff.

Examples from menus (revised frequently): *chicken in lightly curried mayonnaise garnished with bacon lardons & toasted cashews; baked brie with almonds in Cumberland sauce; salmon Balmoral (with prawns in whisky sauce). Lamb Dijonnaise; fillet steak with oyster mushrooms, cream & brandy; calves' liver giradet; grilled breast of barbary duck with oranges & Cointreau; pancake stuffed with rice, spinach & chestnuts in mushroom sauce. Cream-filled hot profiteroles with chocolate sauce; lemon posset.*

Saffron is the world's most expensive spice, and this pleasant little town was once the centre of trade. Also highly valued but far from expensive (less than pub prices), 'The Hoops' can be found right in the middle of the main street, and being on the first floor one can reflect on passing street life whilst digesting the best of fresh food prepared to order. Dating from the 14th century and once a pub, informality still prevails - chef patron Ray Morrison prefers it that way, even though he worked in top West End clubs. With his own style of cooking and attention to detail, he and his family have built an excellent reputation over many years, earning a regular spot in national guides. There's no minimum spend, and the wine list is modestly priced. Booking advisable at weekends.

DICKEN'S RESTAURANT

The Green, Wethersfield, nr Braintree. Tel: (01371) 850723

Hours: 12:30 to 2pm Wed - Sun; 7:30 to 9:30pm Wed - Sat.
Credit cards: Mastercard, Visa, Switch.
Price guide: a la carte £21.50, table d'hote £17.50, lunch £7.50 - £15.

Examples from menus (revised continuously according to market): *Mediterranean fish soup with rouille & croutons; crispy fried wonton with spicy mango relish; crispy Peking duck salad. Seasonal game pudding with braised leeks; grilled sea bass on provencal vegetables; ratatouille pancakes with mornay gratin. Baked pear & almond tart on a lime & butterscotch sauce; lemon tart with sauce anglaise; warm chocolate brownies with vanilla ice cream. Trad. Sun. roasts plus alternatives.*

1996 'County Restaurant of the Year' (Good Food Guide), Dicken's is always a hive of activity: regular theme evenings (eg A Taste of Olde England), wine tasting suppers, ladies' lunches, the Pudding Club, cookery demonstrations. Proprietor John Dicken is a regular on national TV, but resists the temptation to hike up prices. He draws on many years of international experience, and perhaps also from his collection of antiquarian cookbooks, to produce dishes of great diversity and originality, using personally selected fresh produce from the day's markets. The building itself would not look out of place on The Mediterranean, but the extraordinary interior is decidedly English, heavily timbered, oak panelled and with a large minstrels' gallery overlooking the dining room.

THE WHITE HART

Gt Yeldham, nr Halstead. Tel: (01787) 237250 Fax: (01787) 238044

Hours: 12 to 2pm, 6:30 to 9:45pm, daily.
Credit cards: Mastercard, Visa, Diners, Amex, Switch.
Price guide: a la carte £18.

Examples of bar/restaurant meals (lunch & evening, 7 days): *chicken liver paté with toasted brioche; Thai mussels with lemon grass, coriander & green chillies; duck confit terrine with haricot bean puree & pickled beetroot. Braised oxtail with mashed potato; tenderloin of pork with red cabbage & apple & Calvados sauce; tagliatelle with pesto sauce, parmesan cheese & tomato & red onion salad. Rich chestnut terrine with chocolate sauce; blackberry & apple crumble with creme fraiche; creme caramel with prunes poached in liqueur muscat. Trad. Sun. roasts.*

Long admired as one of East Anglia's finest Tudor houses, The White Hart is now also marked as amongst its leading pub-cum-restaurants, having recently been acquired by the Huntsbridge Group (Old Bridge, Huntingdon; Pheasant, Keyston; Three Horseshoes, Madingley). Apart from high standards, there's no group 'formula': chef patron Roger Jones has free reign to develop a distinctive style, augmented by regional theme evenings (eg Tuscany, Piedmont). A common feature, though, is an outstanding wine list. One may dine in bar and restaurant; the atmosphere throughout is very special. Small functions and wedding receptions catered for. Large garden.

FREDERICK'S RESTAURANT

The White House, 32 High Street, Halstead. Tel: (01787) 472729 Fax: (01787) 472806

Hours: 12 to 2pm, 7 to 10pm, Tues - Fri; Sat 7pm onwards, Sun 12pm onwards.
Credit cards: Mastercard, Visa, Diners, Amex, Switch, Delta, Electron.
Price guide: a la carte £22, table d'hote lunch £10.50 & £13.50 (2 & 3 courses).
Accommodation: 1 sngl, 3 dbls/twins; 2 with bathrooms, all with TV,
hair dryer, tea & coff.

Examples from menus (revised every 2-3 weeks): *pan-fried shellfish & fish cakes on delicate saffron & cream sauce; confit of duck on bed of mushy peas with shallot gravy; goats' cheese bruschetta. French onion tartlet topped with avocado & melted brie; roast halibut on bed of spinach with sour cream & lime sauce & tomato & coriander curry chutney; pork fillet stuffed with apricots, sultanas & dates with calvados cream sauce. Chocolate sponge topped with white & dark chocolate mousse; lemon, sultana & ricotta cheese tartlet; iced raspberry parfait with tuille biscuit curls. Trad. Sun. roasts plus alternatives (£12.50 for 3 courses plus coffee).*

Take your time; the table is yours for the evening. Proprietor (since Feb '94) Paul Lofthouse likes his guests to feel completely at ease, better to savour the talents of chef Alex Clucas. And the two beautiful dining rooms (one no-smoking) are conducive to a memorable meal: pastel yellow walls, blue chairs (well spaced), white linen, exposed brickwork and wonderful old timbers. This 450-year-old former merchant's house is one of the very finest of its kind, ornate and wonderfully proportioned - including the rear function room (which opens on to the garden) and the newly refurbished bedrooms. Easy parking on road.

BAUMANN'S BRASSERIE
4/6 Stoneham Street, Coggeshall. Tel: (01376) 561453 Fax: (01376) 563762

Hours: 12:30 to 2pm, 7:30 to 10p daily, except Sat lunch, Sun
evening & all day Mon.
Credit cards: Mastercard, Visa, Amex, Switch, Delta.
Price guide: a la carte £20; lunch £7.50, £9.95 & £12.50
(1, 2 & 3 courses, plus coffee).

Examples from menus (revised 2-monthly): *Black Forest bacon & egg salad with toasted pine nuts in Dijon dressing; creamy leek, potato & onion soup with smoked haddock & rouille croutons; grilled goats' cheese with curried guacamole & blistered peppers. Fresh fish menu eg grilled fillet of sea bass with 3-pepper salsa in lime champagne sauce; honey-basted goose with stewed peaches in red wine juices; traditional toad-in-the-hole. White chocolate truffle cake with cherry compote; prune & Armagnac tart with vanilla ice cream; lemon chiffon mousse in brandysnap basket with stewed fruit. Trad. Sun. roasts £15.95 (4 courses plus coffee).*

Eating out should be fun, never intimidating. Mark Baumann's unstuffy, continental-style brasserie bustles with atmosphere, aided by a a colourful gallery of original paintings, stripped wood floor, unmatching chairs and individual tables. Mark, trained at the Royal Champagne in France, has cooked for royalty and many other VIP's, and his kitchen's creations have won acclaim from national TV, newspapers and food guides. But there are no airs and graces, and prices are extraordinarily modest for a restaurant of such repute. Naturally all is fresh and cooked to order, and for extra interest some Friday evenings are special: could be Australian, American for example, and usually with live music. Available for Saturday weddings etc. Easy parking opposite.

NORTH HILL EXCHANGE BRASSERIE
19-20 North Hill, Colchester. Tel: (01206) 769988 Fax: (01206) 766898

Hours: 11am to 2pm, 6:30pm to 10pm, Mon - Sat.
Credit cards: Mastercard, Visa, Diners, Amex.
Price guide: a la carte £20; lunch £5, £7.50, £9.95 (1, 2, 3 courses).

Examples from menus (revised 6-weekly): *baked filo pastry parcels crammed with prawns & leeks on dill butter sauce; grilled chestnut sausages on celeriac mash; boned & roasted quail on salad of haricot beans & cracked hazelnuts. Fresh fish of the day eg grilled halibut with tomatoes & herbs; roast loin of wild venison with redcurrant juices & red cabbage; layers of aubergine stuffed with courgettes & mozarella. Rum & raisin pudding with hot fudge sauce; passion fruit tart with crushed mango coulis; apricot creme brulée with almond biscuits.*

The brasserie concept is borrowed from France, but many would argue that England has surpassed the continent - North Hill Exchange is evidence of this. Chef proprietor Doug Wright worked in top French and London restaurants, as well as Hintlesham Hall, before setting up in this fine town-centre Georgian building in 1994. Much bigger inside than is first apparent, the dining areas (some no-smoking) are light and easy going, with fine mahogany floors and a much admired art collection. The musical arts play an important role in an exciting diary of events, usually on the last Friday of the month - Booze, Blues Bangers & Mash and Australian Tucker are recent examples. Fresh local market produce painstakingly prepared is always de rigueur in the kitchen. Large upstairs room available for private functions. NCP carpark nearby.

THE WAREHOUSE BRASSERIE
Chapel Street North, Colchester. Tel: (01206) 765656

Hours: 12 to 2pm, 7 to 10pm, daily except Sun evenings.
Credit cards: Mastercard, Visa, Amex, Delta, Switch.
Price guide: a la carte £14 - 17; lunch £8.95 & £10.95 (2 & 3 courses).

Examples from menus (revised monthly): *smoked haddock Florentine tart; field mushrooms stuffed with provence herbs & gruyere cheese; bacon & boudin salad. Grilled seafood brochette; pan-fried cod fillet with saffron & spinach bubble & squeak; best end of spring lamb roasted & served with coriander jus; twice-baked goats' cheese soufflé with roasted red pepper coulis; chargrilled haunch of venison with red wine & field mushroom sauce. Sticky pear & walnut pudding with vanilla ice cream; raspberry vacherin; home-made pistachio ice cream. Trad. Sun. roasts.*

"Best Restaurant in Essex" (Good Food Guide 1990, '94, '95); just yards to the south of the city centre (by Headgate), this former warehouse also benefits from enthusiastic local approbation, and that of Michelin and Egon Ronay. Painted in bold reds and greens, with wooden floors and lively decor, this galleried former warehouse fairly buzzes with an informal atmosphere, as befits the best kind of town centre brasserie. There's no obilgation to eat three courses - if you just fancy a snack with a glass of wine, that's fine. But if you have an appetite, don't miss the seasonal Gourmet Evenings. Prices are surprisingly modest, and that extends to the wine list. Children welcome. Parking in St John's multi-story carpark.

MALTRAVERS RESTAURANT
Clacton Road, Elmstead Market, nr Colchester. Tel: (01206) 822419

Hours: 7 to 9:30 Tues - Sat (to 10pm Fri & Sat); lunch by arrangement
for private parties of 10+ weekdays, 25+ weekends.
Credit cards: Mastercard, Visa, Switch.
Price guide: a la carte £19.

Examples from menus (revised seasonally, plus specials): *crab & pesto savoury prof-iteroles with tomato & sweet pepper sauce; devilled lambs' kidneys on potato pancakes; rabbit & bacon pastie with apple & coriander compote; camembert & cranberry filo puffs with Cumberland sauce. Four-fish pie; smoked haddock & scallop butter tart, glazed with cheese, on saffron cream sauce; breast of chicken stuffed with brie, apples & shallots, with Calvados cream sauce; rack of lamb Nicoise. Brandy snap baskets filled with home-made brandy mousse ice; bread & butter pudding with brandy; hazelnut, praline cream & crisp chocolate layered meringue torte.*

Customers keep coming back after 19 years - a more eloquent testimonial than any guidebook's. Such a consistent 'track record' is possible only by having one chef over all that time: Kathy Oton - she and husband Pepe (who hails from Gibraltar) are also the proprietors. With around eight or nine starters and a dozen main courses (all fresh and home-made, of course), choice could hardly be described as limited, but Kathy's versatility is further demonstrated on regular Gourmet Dinners (£19.25 for six courses plus coffee), or special midweek features like Taste of France (£12.95 for three courses plus coffee). Ask to go on the mailing list. The three dining areas, divided by timber lattices, are very cosy and cottagey, with a rather nice open fire, antiques and flowers. Customers are requested to smoke only in the bar. Unusual wines, also modestly priced.

THE PIER RESTAURANT & HOTEL

The Quay, Harwich. Tel: (01255) 241212 Fax: (01255) 551922

Hours: 12 to 2pm, 6 to 9:30pm daily.
Credit cards: Mastercard, Visa, Diners, Amex, Switch, Collect, Delta.
Price guide: a la carte £25, set price dinner £14.50 & £18 (2 & 3 courses);
lunch £10.50 & £14 (2 & 3 courses); Sun. lunch £16.50; all subject
to 10% service charge; Ha'penny Pier Bistro a la carte £11.50.
Accommodation: 6 dbls/twins (2 may be used as family); all en suite, TV, phone,
tea & coffee, hair dryer on request; from £52.50 - £85; special
2-night break £180 per room (incl. £17.50pp dinner allowance).

Examples from menus (restaurant revised twice-monthly): *terrine of fresh scallops, crab & smoked salmon with herb & lime mayonnaise; rock oysters; gazpacho. Chef's fish pie; ragout of seafood; grilled lobster with bearnaise sauce; entrecote steak 'Helda'; escalope of pork tenderloin 'cordon bleu'. Drambuie bavarois; dark Belgian chocolate parfait glace on white chocolate sauce; summer pudding terrine.* Ha'penny Pier Bistro: *stilton & celery fritters; fish & chips (speciality); fish pie; cajun chicken; steaks.*

You could watch the seafood being landed on the quay on its very short journey to table, via chef/manager (for 19 years) Chris Oakley - one reason why this is one of the most celebrated restaurants in the area. Good, simple and inexpensive snacks may be had in the downstairs bistro. The view is always stunning, especially from the upstairs restaurant, but the nautical decor (a rich marine blue being the theme colour) is also diverting. None of the Victorian grandeur has been lost, and such a strangely quiet location (the town's narrow streets just to the rear) is a marvellous spot for an overnight stay or function (up to 80).

LE TALBOOTH

Gun Hill, Dedham, nr Colchester. Tel: (01206) 323150 Fax: (01206) 322309

Hours: 12 to 2pm, 7 to 9pm daily.
Credit cards: Mastercard, Visa, Amex, Diners.
Price guide: a la carte £35; table d'hote £20 & £23.50 (2 & 3 courses);
lunch £16 & £18.50 (2 & 3 courses). 10% service charge.
Accommodation: 10 luxurious suites at nearby Maison Talbooth (transport provided).

Examples from menus (revised two-monthly, table d'hote weekly): *terrine of salmon & sole layered with tomatoes & coriander, lemon dressing; avocado & white beans, bound with creme fraiche, topped with brown shrimps, bacon vinaigrette; gorgonzola tortellinis with watercress cream & parmesan shavings. Baked monkfish with lemon & thyme crust, cider sauce; individual steak & kidney pudding; peppered barabary duck breast sliced pink on caramelised shallot tart, fragrant orange juice. Oat & honey parfait on apple & cinammon tart; lemon chiffon pie with orange-scented anglaise sauce; creme caramel with strawberries.*

Now in its 46th year (all of them in the hands of the Milsom family), Le Talbooth is amongst England's most widely known and venerated restaurants. It is also one of the most depicted, being a stunning Tudor building beautifully situated on the banks of the River Stour in the heart of Constable Country. To sit out on the terrace under giant parasols is one of the joys of summer. Log fires are winter's compensation, but the marvellous floodlit views can be enjoyed at any time. The menus afford a wide diversity to suit all palates, and prices are not unreasonable for a restaurant of this calibre. Spoil yourself further with a stay at the nearby Maison Talbooth - you won't forget it. You may also like to try the popular seafood restaurant The Pier at Harwich (qv), also owned by the family.

THE OLD BOOT HOUSE RESTAURANT
Main Road, Shotley. Tel: (01473) 787755
NB: not to be confused with The Boot public house at Freston.

Hours: 12 to 2pm, 7pm onwards, daily except Sun evenings &
all day Mondays; booking required.
Credit cards: Mastercard, Visa.
Price guide: a la carte £17 - £20; lunch from £3.95.

Examples from menus (revised daily): *medley of potted rabbit & smoked goose with home-made piccalillli & red cabbage; fresh East Coast crab & farmhouse cheddar omelette; fresh pasta noodles with avocado pear & roasted walnut sauce. Grilled breast of chicken with fresh scallops & smoked bacon; grilled lamb tenderloin with fresh mint & mustard seeds; deep-fried morcels of seafood with elderflower sauce; fresh asparagus quiche with butter sauce. Strawberry & rose petal tartlet; layered milk, white & dark chocolate terrine; exotic fruit salad with light honeysuckle & mint syrup.*

It's like visiting a friend's home; this querky, idiosyncratic restaurant is not an open house - guests are requested to book, but they are in for a rare treat. A very personal service is matched by menus with a country theme, written daily on a whim according to what chef proprietor Ian Chamberlain or wife Pamela have picked that day: could be samphire from the river; wild mushrooms; roses, honeysuckle, lavender or elder from the garden. They even make their own ice cream, bread, pickles and chutneys. You could be lucky and find yourself at a surprise Gourmet Evening (never advertised), where maybe 10 courses are served. Wines, too, are highly individual; those with hand-written labels are brought from France by the vintner herself. Many are available by the glass, including six pudding wines.

SCOTT'S BRASSERIE
4a Orwell Place, Ipswich. Tel: (01473) 230254 Fax: (01473) 218851

Hours: 12 to 2:30pm Mon - Fri; 6:30 to 10pm Tues - Sat.
Credit cards: Mastercard, Visa, Diners, Amex, Switch.
Price guide: set price menu (with chef's daily specials) £14.95 & £17.95
(2 & 3 courses); bistro from £4.95.

Examples from menus (revised three-monthly plus weekly specials): *Bermuda fish chowder; baked Suffolk pheasant terrine; oyster Rockefeller parcels; sun-dried tomato, black olive & basil paté. Smoked haddock & salmon cakes with creme fraiche tartar sauce; baked breast of chicken filled with stilton & coated in grain mustard & cream sauce; marinated tenderloin of lamb skewer on minted couscous. Blackberry & mascarpone creme brulée; chocolate mousse cake; bread & butter pudding with whisky & caramel sauce.* Bistro: *grilled chicken, bacon & brie baguette; traditional Caesar salad; pasta & vegetarian dishes of the day.*

It requires a sure touch to strike a balance between bistro-style informality - suitable for shoppers and business lunches - and a sense of occasion for diners out to celebrate. Scott's carries it off with aplomb. In part this is possible because of the building: much bigger than it looks, it is on three levels, all the rooms being beautifully proportioned; the vaulted wood ceiling of the gallery is particularly striking. The 15 years spent in Bermuda by the eponymous Scott are also clearly an influence, not only on the menu but also that combination of style and relaxed informality. A wide selection of wines, eight of them by the glass, are, like the food, very reasonably priced. Close to shopping centre, within yards of Foundation Street and Cox Lane car parks.

THE RED ONION BISTRO
Ballingdon Street, Sudbury. Tel: (01787) 376777

Hours: 12 to 2pm, 6:30 to 9:30pm Mon - Sat (to 10pm Fri & Sat).
Credit cards: Mastercard, Visa, Switch, Delta.
Price guide: a la carte dinner £15, set price £9.75 (3 courses); lunch a la carte
£12, set price £5.75 & £7.50 (2 & 3 courses).

Examples from menus (revised daily): *baked fresh crab terrine with honey & grape-fruit dressing; duck & pork rillette; mushroom & gruyere croustade. Deep-fried smoked haddock & prawn fishcakes; home-made seafood sausages; baked spicy meat-loaf with pizzaiola sauce; griddled chicken breast with tarragon & sherry vinegar sauce; home-made rumpburger with garlic butter; baked risotto stuffed peppers; blackboard specials. Vanilla cream with peach & prune compote; fresh raspberry tart; chocolate & vanilla parfait.*

The common perception that pubs are always cheaper than restaurants is well and truly scotched here at the south end of Sudbury. £7.50 for a three-course meal is stagger-ingly good value, especially given waiter service and the undoubted quality of chef Darren Boyles' cooking (lauded in most of the major guides). The bold use of strong colours, stripped wood floors, tables partitioned off and a warm informality will be instantly recognisable to the many who frequented Gerry and Jane Ford's previous ventures, Ford's in Sudbury and The Warehouse, Colchester (qv). Here there is also a long club table, newspapers provided, able to seat 14, no bookings taken. A clever innovation: guests are invited into the cellar to choose from a range of fine wines (sev-eral in half bottles), including many bin ends at prices lower than one would pay in a shop. The quality house wines are just £6.95. Pleasant under-cover courtyard garden.

SCUTCHER'S BISTRO

Westgate Street, Long Melford. Tel: (01787) 310200

Hours: 12 to 2pm, 7 to 9:30pm Tues. - Sat.
Credit cards: Mastercard, Visa, Amex, Switch.
Price guide: a la carte £20.

Examples from menu (revised monthly): *seized scallops & crayfish on spicy salsa; toasted goats' cheese & potato terrine with caper & red onion salad; sautéd foie gras on pea purée with caramelised shallot sauce. Poached fillet of turbot with broad beans, peas & bacon, vermouth sauce; roasted fllet of lamb on spinach, lemon cream flavoured with garlic & mint; cheesy risotto with oyster mushrooms & asparagus topped with poached egg. Rich chocolate tart with orange custard; burnt lemon cream with fresh raspberries; fluffy pancakes with compote of cherries & clotted ice cream. Blackboard specials from daily market.*

Twice featured on regional television, lauded annually by the main national guides, Nicholas and Diane Barrett run one of the most universally respected restaurants in the region, with an informal 'bistro' style of cooking and presentation, at very modest prices. Over 100 wines are listed from all over the world, starting from just £7.90 for house wine, the most expensive being only £26. They completely gutted this former pub (The Scutcher's Arms), but were careful not to lose touch with its ancient origins. Split-level tiled floors, farmhouse furniture, pretty floral wall coverings and curtains, inglenook fireplace and a forest of oak beams make for a refreshingly light and pleasant environment. Equally important, the washrooms are unashamedly luxurious!

THE SWAN HOTEL

High Street, Lavenham. Tel: (01787) 247477 Fax: (01787) 248286

Hours: 12 to 2pm, 7 to 9pm (9:30pm Fri & Sat), daily; sandwiches available
all day in lounge bar; morning coffees & afternoon teas.
Credit cards: Mastercard, Visa, Amex, Diners, Switch, Delta, Forte Goldcard.
Price guide: a la carte £35; bar lunches c. £10, snacks from £3.
Accommodation: 7 sngls (£75), 37 dbls/twins (from £120), 2 suites (£145);
some 4-posters, all en-suite, TV, phone, hair-dryer, trouser press,
tea & coff; special weekend breaks.

Examples from menus (revised seasonally): *fresh scallops wrapped in smoked salmon with citrus dressing; mille feuille of duck foie gras layered with celeriac, apple rosti & marinated artichokes. Seared fillet of Dover sole & tiger prawns with chive butter sauce; breast of guinea fowl with sun-dried apricots & pistachio forcemeat; veal cutlet with oyster mushrooms & tarragon sauce. Grand Marnier soufflé glace; summer pudding; pecan pie with vanilla ice cream & sauce anglais. Trad. Sun. roasts.*

One of Britain's most illustrious hotels, this magnificent 14th-century inn is exceptional even in historic Lavenham, with which it is synonymous. Yet one never feels intimidated; quite the reverse - guests comment that it is a home-from-home, not at all starchy, and one can savour its special atmosphere at very modest cost. The restaurant and three function rooms are particularly jaw-dropping, and now having a licence, would make a memorable backdrop to a wedding. In a surprising four acres there's room for two car parks and lovely gardens with croquet lawn. Ask about medieval nights, murder mystery weekends and the popular 'Music at Leisure', featuring well known performers. Try also the sister hotel, The Bull at nearby Long Melford.

THE GRANGE HOTEL & RESTAURANT
Barton Road, Thurston, Bury St Edmunds. Tel: (01359) 231260

Hours: 12 to 2pm, 7 to 10pm (9pm Sundays) daily.
Credit cards: Mastercard, Visa.
Price guide: a la carte £16, Sunday lunch £11.25, bar snacks from £3.75.
Accommodation: 2 sngls (£37-£42), 10 dbls/twins (£50-£69), 1 family; all en-suite, TV, phone, hair-dryer, tea & coff. Special breaks: 2 nights dinner, b & b £75pp.

Examples from menus (revised seasonally): *pork & chicken liver terrine with tangy Cumberland sauce; button mushrooms with herb & garlic-flavoured stuffing, topped with white sauce & gratinated. Half a Suffolk roast duckling with sweet & sour sauce flavoured with apricot, spring onion & ginger; vegetarian fricassée; four lamb cutlets pan-fried with rosemary & sherry jus, garnished with pan-fried polenta. Summer pudding; lemon & ginger crunch; chocolate roulade. Trad. Sun. roasts.*

For three generations a family-run business, this beautifully proportioned mock-Tudor mansion stands in splendid isolation, hidden behind tall trees in two acres of parkland and garden. Aproaching via the long, tree-lined drive, the visitor leaves the madness of the A14 a mile behind, trading it for a saner world of sedate pleasures. The tone is set by the panelled entrance lobby, and a beautiful Adam fireplace graces the dignified restaurant. Two lounge bars look out over a south-facing terrace, from where many a wedding party has spilled onto the large lawn - a wonderful setting for such an occasion. The proprietor is also trained chef and wine buff; he prepares classic Anglo-French dishes at extraordinarily reasonable prices. Ideally placed for the region's attractions and a range of country sports.

THE REGENCY RESTAURANT
AT THE ANGEL HOTEL

Angel Hill, Bury St Edmunds. Tel: (01284) 753926 Fax: (01284) 750092

Hours: 12:30 to 2pm, 7 to 10pm, daily.
Credit cards: Mastercard, Visa, Diners, Amex.
Price guide: a la carte £25, table d'hote £19.50, lunch £16.50.
Accommodation: 11 sngls (from £62), 26 dbls/twins (from £72), 4 family, 1 suite;
individually designed, some 4- posters; all en- suite, TV, hair dryer,
trouser press; weekend breaks from £38pp per night.

Examples from menus (revised monthly): *smoked trout mousse flavoured with vodka, served with slices of fresh grapefruit; green Regency salad (asparagus, mixed herbs, diced avocado, french beans); gnocchi tossed in olive oil, garnished with sun-dried tomatoes & roasted peppers. Thinly sliced salmon on bed of fennel flavoured with Pernod; breast of guinea fowl with spring greens & sweet pickle bacon sauce; globe artichoke filled with ragout of tomato, mozzarella & mushrooms, finished with dash of olive oil & basil. Pistachio steamed pudding; lemon & lime tart; raspberry soufflé glacé. Trad. Sun. roasts.*

The Angel is synonymous with Bury St Edmunds; the relationship goes back a far as 1452. Once a celebrated coaching inn, Charles Dickens wrote part of The Pickwick Papers during his two visits. Many other great names have stayed here over the centuries, including royalty. The refinement which they enjoyed can be yours at a very affordable price, and this goes for the stylish, elegant Regency Restaurant, overlooking the ancient abbey with its lovely riverside gardens. This stands on merit as one of the finest restaurants in the area, witnessed by the AA two rosettes for fine food and service.

THE VAULTS AT THE ANGEL HOTEL
Angel Hill, Bury St Edmunds. Tel: (01284) 753926 Fax: (01284) 750092

Hours: 12:00 to 2pm, 6.30 to 10pm, daily.
Credit cards: Mastercard, Visa, Diners, Amex.
Price guide: starters from £3-95 main courses from £7
Accommodation: 11 sngls (from (£62), 26 dbls/twins (from £72), 4 family, 1 suite;
all individually designed, some 4-posters; all en-suite, TV, hair dryer,
trouser press; weekend breaks from £38pp per night.

Examples from menus (revised monthly): *Thai salmon fishcake set on a herb salad; smoked seafood pasta; provencal tartlet prepared with cheese and Mediterranean-style vegetables; braised lamb shank infused with root vegetables; breast of chicken filled with spinach and hazelnut and served with a wild mushroom sauce; char-grilled tuna steak marinated in lime and chilli, presented with rocket leaves; 'Dorchester' chocolate and ginger pudding; strawberry creme brulée.*

The vaulted arches of the ancient crypt, said to be part of the 12th-century abbey, provide a unique medieval setting to a modern brasserie-style restaurant, and marvellous accoustics for the regular Jazz Evenings and other live entertainment throughout the year. The hotel welcomes children (and permits pets). Excellent facilities for business and private functions. Experienced manager Jolyon Gough is formerly of the famous George at Stamford and Oakley Court, Windsor.

THE OLD COUNTING HOUSE
RESTAURANT & BAR

Haughley, nr. Stowmarket IP14 3NR   Tel & Fax: (01449) 673617

Hours: from 12 noon Mon - Fri. and from 7:15pm Mon -Sat.
Credit cards: Mastercard, Visa, Diners, Amex.
Price guide: table d'hote lunch £12.75 & £15 (2 & 3 courses & coff.);
dinner £22.50 (4 courses & coff.). Bistro menu starters
from £2.95, main courses from £7.50.

Examples from menus (revised 3-weekly): *Mediterranean tartlet; salmon brochette with tomato & onion salsa; goats' cheese salad. Kidney cassolet in rich dark port sauce; tuna with lime & coriander; trio of roast vegetables with herb stuffing on fresh tomato sauce. Fresh fruits with hot chocolate dip; vanilla bavarois with compote of berries; pear & almond tart; cheese aigrettes.* Bar: *tagliatelle with smoked salmon; crispy trout fillet with breadrumbs & almond; chicken liver salad; sirloin steak.*

The common perception that pubs are always cheaper than restaurants is increasingly ill founded. So too is the notion that the latter are for special occasions only. With a new licence, proprietors Paul and Susan (the chef) Woods now also have a bar, where guests are welcome to drop in for a drink in the civilised surroundings of this marvellous 13th-century building, and maybe enjoy a good, simple meal at prices comparable to any pub. On the last Friday of each month intriguing theme evenings - Pink & White is one recent example - are very popular, as are the live Jazz Nights (details on request). This historic village, a regular winner of 'Anglia in Bloom', is also distinguished by its medieval street, the finest Motte & Bailey in the region, and a church with only five bells (not the usual six) and leather fire buckets still hanging in the tower. Les Routiers and AA recommended. Easy parking.

THE CAPTAIN'S TABLE SEAFOOD RESTAURANT
3 Quay Street, Woodbridge. Tel: (01394) 383145

Hours: lunch & dinner Tues - Sat; 'bar' meals lunchtime and
midweek evenings; closed Sundays & Mondays.
Credit cards: Mastercard, Visa, Diners, Amex, Switch.
Price guide: a la carte £19.50, table d'hote £15.50 (3 courses), snacks from £3.25.

Examples from menus (revised frequently): *profiteroles filled with smoked seafood with coriander sauce; terrine of avocado & smoked turkey; local oysters. Coquillage of local fish & shellfish in cheese & sherry sauce; lemon sole fillets filled with prawns in a seafood & ginger sauce; baked aubergine (filled with courgettes, cashew nuts, tomato & basil topped with cheese); sirloin steak. Grand Marnier choc pot; treacle tart with cream; homemade ice creams. Bar meals and daily blackboard specials.*

"According to wind and tide, fisherman's fancy, farmer's whim and gardener's back" - the caveat on the menu (supplemented by a blackboard) is a clue to the fresh provenance upon which diners have been able to rely for nearly 30 years. That's how long Tony Prentice has been running his ever-popular restaurant in one of the region's most attractive and interesting small towns. Yachtsman will often make their way from the quayside straight to The Captains's Table for further communion with the sea and its bounty, although landlubbers are equally keen. The maritime atmosphere is contrived by the felicitous use of fishing nets, seascapes and nautical oddities, including an old diving helmet. The wine list is large and of seriously high quality (not overpriced). If seafood is not your first choice, the vegetarian and meat alternatives are much more than mere afterthought.

THE RIVERSIDE RESTAURANT
Quayside, Woodbridge. Tel: (01394) 382587 Fax: (01394) 382656

Hours: lunch 12 to 2:30pm, Dinner 6 to 10:30pm, daily except Sun. evenings.
Credit cards: Mastercard, Visa, Amex.
Price guide: a la carte £15 - £20, dinner & film package £19. Light lunch from £3.95.

Examples from a la carte (revised seasonally): *hot chicken liver salad with mayonnaise; special platter for 2 - generous selection of hot & cold hors d'oeuvres. Half a crispy roast duck cooked Chinese-style & served with orange & ginger sauce; fresh grilled tuna with rosemary & garlic; Scottish salmon in filo pastry with spinach & seaweed in lobster sauce. Celebrated homemade puddings eg hot toffee pudding with cream or ice cream; terrine of three chocolates with noisette sauce; pancake parcel filled with curacao souffle or rich double chocolate & praline mousse.*

The Riverside is part of a unique complex containing the luxurious 288-seater theatre/cinema, one of the leading independents in the country. It is thus able to offer a special three-course Dinner and Film package for only £19, plus the exciting a la carte. The airy garden-style restaurant, flooded with light by day, becomes magical at night by candlelight. Enjoy pre-film/theatre drinks in the atmospheric bar, with its antique theatrical mirror and array of old filmstar photographs, while you choose from the Dinner & Film menu, eating before or after the film of your choice. The friendly staff and culinary skills of Vincent Jeffers (head chef) also make for a night to remember. In summer stroll by the Riverside and discover the delights of the ornate gazebo: ice cream, French crepes, cappuccino or espresso coffee, to enjoy under the continental-style canopy. Whatever your choice, you will find proprietor Stuart Saunders true to his word: "The best is not always the most expensive."

HEDGEHOGS

Main A12, Kelsale, nr Saxmundham. Tel: (01728) 604444 Fax: (01728) 604499

Hours: 12 to 1:30pm, 7 to 9:30pm Tues - Sat; 12 to 2pm Sun.
Mondays by prior arrangement only.
Credit cards: Mastercard, Visa, Amex, Switch, Delta.
Price guide: a la carte £16, table d'hote £9.50, lunch £7.50
(2 courses from blackboard).

Examples from menus (revised seasonally): *smoked sprats with spicy tomato & coriander salsa; sweet onion & ricotta tart; crispy courgettes with hot bacon salad & garlic dip. Grilled sea bass with saffron & olive risotto; roast shank of lamb with chunky onion sauce; confit of duck served crisp with pea & lovage purée; specials eg cheese soufflé with Greek salad, roast hock of pork in Szechuan pepper. Own-baked waffles with hot toffee bananas & ice cream; home-made Greek baclava; Hedgehog's sticky toffee pudding (noted - available to take away). Trad. Sun. roasts.*

The name was chosen when a nest of the endearing little creatures was uncovered during renovations. They were safely rehoused, and we are left with a building of extraordinary character and atmosphere, with low ceilings, a floor on what seems like a 1-in-8 gradient, magnificent fireplaces, timbers, brickwork, and everywhere you look cuddly toy hedgehogs in period costume - a marvellous venue for a wedding (or conference up to 20), with a nice garden in which to spill out. Taking his lead from the likes of Raymond Blanc, Albert Roux and others, chef proprietor (since 1995) Stephen Yare presents refreshingly different menus and a programme of theme nights, such as Tapas, Italian, Starters & Pudding Club (a regular), plus cookery demonstrations. Outside catering and bar service.

THE SWAN HOTEL

Market Place, Southwold. Tel: (01502) 722186 Fax: (01502) 724800

Hours: 12 to 1:45pm, 7 to 9:30pm, 7 days; Bar Meals 12 to 2:30pm
(3pm Sats), 7 days.
Credit cards: Mastercard, Visa, Diners, Amex, Switch.
Price guide: 3 daily set dinner menus: £21, £27.50, £33. Lunch £13.50 (2 courses),
£15.50 (3 courses); Sunday lunch £15.50 & £17.50 (2 & 3 courses).
Accommodation: 5 singles (from £48), 38 doubles/twins (from £86), 2 suites
(from £145). Midweek winter breaks (from £55 pp) incl.
3-course dinner with coffee, b & b.

Examples from menus (changed daily): *Scottish salmon fishcakes with lemon butter sauce; pressed duck & cassoulet terrine, balsamic jus; gateau of honey-roasted parsnips & plum tomatoes with a goats' cheese glaze; rosettes of lamb with champ-valon potatoes & rosemary jus; roast loin of Adnams' Pork, chateau potatoes; sautéed pigeon breasts stuffed with foie gras, wrapped in apple sauce savoy cabage; Cajun-style ragout of seafood (scallops, tuna, king prawns & salmon) with turmeric rice. Summer berry pudding & clotted cream; roasted banana & chocolate crumble; orange & basil creme brulée (to name just a few!).*

Southwold is one of England's last unspoilt coastal towns, an enchanting throw-back to an age long past, away from the stresses of the modern world. At its heart is this classic 17th-century hotel, remodelled in the 1820s, and the period refinement and elegance has not been lost to more recent modernisations. Like all the public rooms, the dining room is beautifully furnished, and serves as well for a function as a private dinner for two. The smaller informal Trellis Room, overlooking a tiny courtyard, is used as an extension or for private parties. Three fixed price menus offer a very considerable choice, ranging from English classics to some highly original eclectic suggestions from Chef de Cuisine Chris Coubrough. He very much favours fresh seasonal produce, using home-grown herbs and own-baked bread. Simpler but still excellent fare is available in the bar, accompanied by an award winning Adnams' ale, or perhaps a wine from the celebrated Adnams' range - Wine Merchants of the Year in 1992,1993 and 1995. Afternoon teas are another timeless tradition well observed. Bedrooms are very well appointed, individually decorated, and have colour televisions, direct telephones and hair-dryers. Whilst every latest facility is there, the management (led by Carole Ladd) takes pride in the fact that the hotel continues to provide the very best in ambience, friendly courteous service and first class products. Widely acclaimed in the national press and magazines, this hotel not only serves the needs of one looking for a restful haven of peace, but also the tired business person seeking to relax from a stressful day, or hold an informal business meeting without the interruptions of modern office technology and continous noise of telephones.

THE CROWN HOTEL
High Street, Southwold. Tel: (01502) 722275 Fax: (01502) 727263

Hours: 12:30 to 1:30pm, 7:30 to 9:30pm, 7 days; Bar meals 12:15 to 2pm,
7 to 9:30pm, 7 days.
Credit cards: Mastercard, Visa, Amex, Diners.
Price guide: set price £21.50; lunch £16.25; bar meals from £2.95 - £12.50.
Accommodation: 2 singles (£43), 8 doubles/twins (£65), 1 family (£90),
all with private facilities.

Examples from restaurant menus (changed daily): *soused herring fillet, warm butter potatoes, honey & soy dressing; duck liver & pistachio nut parfait with toasted brioche & apple & ginger chutney. Salmon & basil fish cakes with rocket salad & lemon sauce; chargrilled lamb's liver with parsnip mash & red wine & tarragon sauce. Caramelised lemon tart with creme fraiche; iced nougat & black cherry parfait with raspberry purée.*

Feted regularly by national newspapers and major food guides, The Crown enjoys a celebrity well beyond the region. Managed by Anne Simpson, it is a flagship for owners Adnams, whose brewery is near, and whose award-winning range of ales is available in both bars. Being also an esteemed wine merchant, the list is of course exceptional, with nearly 300 wines, 20 available by the glass. But it is as much the food (prepared under the leadership of head chef Simon Reynolds) which wins the plaudits. Its popularity means that booking in the restaurant is always advisable. The essence of an 18th-century coaching inn is still much in evidence - antique furniture, old paintings and carved fireplaces - and the individual bedrooms are simple but attractive. Hotel closed one week in January. Limited parking at rear.

THE CRICKETERS
Wangford Road, Reydon, nr Southwold. Tel: (01502) 723603 Fax: (01502) 722194

Hours: 12 to 2pm, 7 to 9pm daily (bar & restaurant)
Credit cards: Mastercard, Visa.
Price guide: set price £13.50 (3 courses); bar snacks & meals from £3.50.
Accommodation: 10 bedrooms; single £35, dbl £52, family £73.

Examples from restaurant menus (revised daily): *home-made soups; poached halibut steak with mushroom & tarragon sauce; roast baby guinea fowl with Madeira sauce; escalope of pork fillet Sicilian; sauteed lambs' kidneys & mushrooms in red wine sauce.* Bar: *vegetables & pasta baked in creamy cheese sauce topped with toasted almonds; fresh fish; cold meat platters; daily specials. Homemade sweets. Trad. Sun. roasts.*

The Cricketers (formerly The Randolph) has been a centre of rest and recreation since 1892. Recent renovation has clearly enhanced the public rooms, and cricket memorabilia - prints, photographs of local teams, signed bats - adorn the bright yellow walls. The bar and dining room have also been successfully renovated, and above are ten comfortable bedrooms and a light, airy Drawing Room. Over the past seven years or so Teresa Doy (manageress) has earned a firm 'thumbs up' from local clientele, reflected in an ever-increasing volume of business, drawn back by delicious food (cooked by long serving head chef Kevin Ellis) accompanied by the award-winning Adnams ales and wines. Yet more improvements are in the pipeline. Parties of up to 60 can be accommodated in the hotel, many more in marquees on the vast lawn.

THE CROOKED BARN RESTAURANT
Ivy Lane (off A146), Oulton Broad,' Lowestoft.
Tel: (01502) 501353/588144 Fax: (01502) 501539

Hours: 12 to 2pm, 7 to 9:30pm, 7 days.
Credit cards: Mastercard, Visa, Diners, Amex, Switch, Delta.
Price guide: a la carte £26, table d'hote £20, bistro from £5.
Accommodation: 11 dbls/twins, 1 family; all en-suite, TV, hair dryer, tea & coff.,
king-size beds; £65 sngl incl., £79 - £89 dbl; 2-night stays
£52.50pp per night, based on 2 sharing; wheelchair access to rooms;
Tourist Board category 1. S/C apartments also.

Examples from menus (a la carte revised 4-6 months, table d'hote daily): *pan-fried boudin of local chicken & pistachio nuts on bed of baby spinach & red onion marmalade; plate of Italian-style stuffed vegetables. Medley of little fishes, lightly steamed & served in broth of saffron, leeks & fresh dill; roast fillet of English lamb with sweet potato purée flavoured with marjoram, surrounded in flageolet bean & garlic sauce. Duo of white & dark chocolate mousse flavoured with malibou, surrounded in chilled lemon sauce anglais; fresh strawberry & vanilla cheesecake topped with mascarpone. Trad. Sun. roasts.* Bistro: *pan-fried Thai crab cakes; roast fillet of monkfish with salad of couscous & peppers in sweet red pepper sauce; Spanish tortilla of potato, mixed peppers & aubergine served with tomato salsa & tapenade toasts.*

An AA Rosette in the first year of trading is no small achievement; proprietors Paul Coe and Caroline Sterry, together with chef Richard Pye, have brought genuine class to an area that badly needed it. Their conversion of these 18th-century farm buildings was superb: the dining room (formerly a barn) is a magnificent example. Bedrooms are large and well equipped, with some nice touches: two telephone points, magazines provided. It all stands in 40 acres (three of them lovely gardens), home to a flock of rare sheep and a menagerie of other animals, and commanding the best views of Oulton Broad. An outstanding venue for weddings, conferences etc.

THE DE LA POLE ARMS

Wingfield, nr Eye. Tel: (01379) 384545 Fax: (01379) 384377

Hours: 12 to 2pm, 7 to 9pm daily; bar 12 to 2pm, 6:30 to 9:30pm daily
(open 11am to 3pm, 6 to 11pm daily).
Credit cards: Mastercard, Visa.
Price guide: a la carte £22, table d'hote & lunch £14; bar meals from around £5.

Examples from menus (revised 6-monthly): *grilled queen scallops with crispy smoked bacon pieces; terrine of pork, chicken & apricot on bed of red cabbage; salad of 6 fresh fruits. Pan-fried monkfish & mussel in Cajun sauce; roast rack of lamb with rosemary, lime & ginger; timbale of courgette, beef tomato, basil & parmesan in rich provencal sauce. English caramel burnt cream with walnut & maple biscuit; raspberry 'Eton Mess'; capuccino mousse. Trad. Sun. roasts.* Bar: *De la Pole fishcakes; hot seafood bowls; grilled tuna & tartare open sandwich; fish & chips in beer batter; beef in ale; broccoli bake; daily specials eg pork casserole (with apricots & fruit beer), poached haddock with fresh asparagus & light mushroom & cream sauce.*

Lost in the gentle, rolling landscape of the Waveney Valley, the tiny village of Wingfield has three good reasons to seek it out: the famous Wingfield College, open to the public at weekends and with a superb programme of classical music, opera, jazz, lectures etc; the medieval church; and, directly opposite, this beautiful 15th-century inn. Although one is welcome to drop by for one of the outstanding St Peter's local ales, it is as a quality restaurant (specialising in seafood) that this stable mate of The Cornwallis Arms at Brome (qv) is widely appreciated. The photo does not flatter; the interior really is a delight. A little tricky to find, but persistence will be rewarded!

CORNWALLIS ARMS

Brome, nr Eye. Tel: (01379) 870326 Fax: (01379) 870051

Hours: 12 to 2pm, 7 to 9:30pm daily; bar 12 to 2:30pm, 6:30 to 9:30pm daily.
Credit cards: Mastercard, Visa, Diners, Amex, Delta, JCB.
Price guide: a la carte £27, table d'hote £15, lunch £15; bar from about £5
Accommodation: 11 dbls/twins, some 4-posters; all en-suite, TV, mini bar, hair- dryer,
trouser press, tea & coff; from £80 per room; 2 nights champagne
dinner, b & b £140 per person.

Examples from menus (revised 2-monthly): *slices of gravadlax filled with smoked salmon mousse, with dill sauce; sauté of wild pigeon breast, with onions & Norfolk smoked ham. Fresh Dover sole grilled, with lemon & parsley butter; pan-fried duck magret with caramelised orange & pink peppercorn sauce; butter crepes filled with mixed vegetables & woodland mushrooms in saffron sauce, topped with melted cheese.* Bar: *fresh-baked baguettes; venison sausages with mustard gravy & bubble & squeak fritters; steak & kidney suet pudding (noted); oven-roasted cod fillet topped with prawns & cheese. Grand Marnier & marmalade bread & butter pudding; chocolate sponge pudding with milk chocolate sauce; caramel shortbread. Trad. Sun. roasts.*

Approaching through 20 acres of parkland, past magnificent water gardens and topiary, you will be aware that this luxury country house hotel is special. It's one of the region's finest buildings, stretching back 435 years. The public rooms and bedrooms are just superb, but great architecture alone is not enough: under owner (since 1995) George Wortley (an hotelier for 25 years) and experienced head chef Kim Hatch, Cornwallis Arms is also feted by leading national food guides and is well known in the area and beyond. The opulence once reserved only for the wealthy is now yours for the price of a pint in the Tudor Bar - try the range of St Peter's fine ales.

WEAVERS WINE BAR & EATING HOUSE
Market Hill, Diss. Tel: (01379) 642411

Hours: Tues - Fri 12 to 1:30pm, Mon - Sat 7 to 9:30pm; not Christmas.
Credit cards: Mastercard, Visa, Diners, Amex.
Price guide: a la carte £20, table d'hote £13.50 (3 courses),
lunch £7.95 & £10.75 (2 & 3 courses).

Examples from menus (revised weekly): *timbal of smoked salmon filled with crab mousse, served with fresh mango & a kiwi coulis; alligator, smoked bacon, pork & mushroom terrine served with soured cream & beetroot purée. Roast fillet of sea bass set over seasonal salad leaves with red onion marmalade dressing; marinated & roasted tenderloin of pork sliced over pan-fried aubergine, tomatoes & onions, topped with humous; individual steak, kidney & mushroom pie topped with flaky pastry. Baked treacle & ginger sponge with toffee sauce & custard; brown bread ice cream in brandy snap basket.*

The prosperous Weavers' Guild built this as a chapel in the 15th century. The atmosphere today is much more relaxed and convivial, and sustenance is of a less spiritual, more temporal kind. Apart from an excellent range of malt whiskies and wines, fresh, reasonably priced food, flavoured by herbs grown in the garden, is always interesting and unusual, whether for lunch or dinner. Thus has a first rate reputation been established by chef proprietor William Bavin and wife Wilma since they opened in April '87, after having restored the building. From the simple wooden tables, each with a vase of flowers, one can ruminate on the passing street life of this pleasant little town, viewed through large windows.

THE DOVE RESTAURANT
Wortwell, Harleston (on A143 by-pass). Tel: (01986) 788315

Hours: anytime, but booking required.
Credit cards: Mastercard, Visa.
Price guide: a la carte £15 to £25, Sun. lunch £8.50
Accommodation: 3 doubles/twins (2 en suite), £32 dble, £17.50 sngl,
B & B. Tourist Board 2 Crowns Approved.

Examples from menus (revised seasonally): *seafood pancake; melon with curried prawns. Own-recipe venison pie; ragout fruits de mer; scampi Provencal; coquilles St. Jacques; chicken supreme; own-recipe steak & kidney pie; trout; steaks. Crepe maison (pancake filled with raspberries, or orange or lemon, and pastry cream); meringue Chantilly; syllabub; chocolate eclair.*

Simple country restaurants serving honest home-cooked food are among the best reasons for visiting France. However, one need only travel as far as the A143 by-pass near Wortwell (not the village itself) to experience the same pleasure. Chef Patron John Oberhoffer, recipient of the Cordon Culinaire award and the Association Culinaire Francais de Londres winner's medal, is a distinguished practioner of the art of French country cooking. With wife Pat he has over the last 19 years established the Dove as a restaurant respected not just for good food but for the unpretentious manner in which it is presented, and at very reasonable prices. The wine list is mostly French, with some German, but special requests are met when possible. They are also pleased to cater for private parties up to 30, and offer a good breakfast after a night in one of the comfortable bedrooms - you are well placed here in the lovely Waveney Valley for business or pleasure. A 'Dove' has stood on this acre of ground, bordering a stream, since around the time of the French Revolution.

NUMBER 24
24 Middleton Street, Wymondham. Tel: (01953) 607750

Hours: lunch Tues - Sat., dinner from Wed - Sat.
Credit cards: Mastercard, Visa.
Price guide: a la carte dinner £18; lunch main course from £4.95.

Examples from menus (revised fortnightly): *seafood minestrone; cured salmon with blinis; seared scallops with lentils & coriander. Salad nicoise; sauté of chicken with wild mushrooms & Madeira; roasted aubergine with peppered pasta. Chocolate brownie with chocolate malt ice cream; rum & raisin pudding with glazed bananas; coconut waffles with rhubarb compote.*

This popular family-run restaurant goes from strength to strength. Working single-handed in the kitchen, chef proprietor Richard Hughes prepares some of the most innovative dishes around, using local produce, consistently cooked and beautifully presented. As well as recognition from the AA and Egon Ronay, recent accolades include the prestigious 'Menu of the Year', previously bestowed on the likes of the Roux brothers, The Dorchester and Le Talbooth. A regular on Radio Norfolk, columnist in the Caterer & Hotel Keeper and a favourite at many cookery shows around the country, Richard's food is definitely putting Norfolk ingredients on the map! A thriving outside catering business, fine wine dinners and very popular monthly cookery demonstrations mean that the many regulars always have something to look forward to - ask to go on mailing list.

PARK FARM COUNTRY HOTEL
Hethersett, nr Norwich. Tel: (01603) 810264 Fax: (01603) 812104

Hours: 12 to 2pm, 7 to 9:30pm (9pm Sundays); barmeals 12 to 9:30pm
except Sats (12 to 5pm) & Suns (6 to 9pm)
Credit cards: Mastercard, Visa, Diners, Amex, Switch, Delta.
Price guide: a la carte £23, table d'hote dinner £17.50; table d'hote lunch £12.25;
Sun lunch £13.25; bar snacks from £4.
Accommodation: 4 sngls (£65), 29 dbls/twins (from £90), 4 family, 1 suite; all en-suite,
TV, direct phone, tea & coff., some with trouser press, 4-posters &
whirlpool bath; special 2-night breaks.

Examples from menus: *Game sausage celeriac, with apple purée & game sauce; Smoked chicken mousse with cheese wafers. Roasted monkfish with pommery mustard & wild mushrooms; Noisettes of venison wrapped in bacon with redcurrant & port sauce; Asparagus, mushrooms & egg in pastry with spring onion & cream sauce.* Bar: *Plaice mornay; Steak, mushroom & onion pie; Savoury pancake; Mushroom curry; Jacket potatoes; Baguettes; Salads; Sandwiches Children's menu. Home-made sweets, cakes & biscuits.*

A small hotel with a big atmosphere, the facilities as well as the personal touch at this Georgian Hotel would put many larger establishments to shame. The Leisure Club (available to all residents) is impressively equipped with a sizable fitness studio and indoor heated pool. Up to 120 delegates can be seated in the modern conference suite. The restaurant has a reputation for fine cuisine and wines, worth a visit even if not staying. It all stands in beautifully landscaped gardens with a water feature. Recommended by major national guides.

YAXHAM MILL FREEHOUSE & RESTAURANT
Norwich Road, Yaxham, nr E. Dereham Tel: (01362) 693144 Fax: (01362) 858556

Hours: 11:30am to 2:15pm, 7 to 9:45pm daily.
Credit cards: Mastercard, Visa, Switch.
Price guide: a la carte £19; bar meals from £5.95; Sunday lunch
£7.50 & £9.50 (2 & 3 courses).
Accommodation: two 1-bed & two 2-bed cottages, self-contained, also available
for B & B; plus new caravan site.

Examples from menus (revised seasonally): *pan-fried haloumi cheese in breadrumbs & sesame seeds with spinach sauce; baked avocado fiiled with crabmeat & covered in peppercorn sauce. Roasted red snapper in pink berry sauce; vegetable filo pies; duck breast cooked in kiwi & ginger; many daily specials. Belgian chocolate torte; mandarin & ginger roulade; raspberry charlotte russe. Trad. Sun. roasts.* Bar: *steak & kidney pudding with Irish ale; steaks; curry; chilli; deep-fried cod/skate; daily specials eg terrine of pheasant, stilton & mushroom bake. Treacle sponge; bread & butter pudding; summer pudding.*

Built in 1860, the mill stands out like a beacon in the flat lands at the very centre of Norfolk. The well equipped self-catering (or B & B) cottages and caravan site next to it make an excellent base from which to explore the county's many attractions. But since September '96 traffic has been increasingly headed the other way, towards this newish restaurant, revitalised by a local duck farmer, assisted by versatile chef Charles Newcombe, who has cooked for the royal Margarets (Windsor and Thatcher), and new chef Henryk. Business lunches can be prepared quickly, but good food is best lingered over - in two cottagey dining rooms (one a former chapel) with crisp white linen and fresh flowers, or in the pleasant little bar. The good natured staff welcome children, and there's live music every Thursday evening. Barbecues in garden. Outside bar and catering service.

BRASTED'S ON THE PARK
Weston House, Weston Longville. Tel: (01603) 873232

Hours: 12 to 2pm, 7 to 9:30pm daily except Sun. evenings & all day Mons.
Credit cards: Mastercard, Visa.
Price guide: a la carte dinner £23; table d'hote lunch £13.50; bar snacks from £1.60

Examples from menus (revised 2-monthly): *smoked pheasant with pear chutney; roasted Devon scallops with snail butter; assortment of smoked fishes; stilton & celery soup; fine paté of chicken liver. Wild Highland venison with juniper-flavoured sauce; pheasant braised in red wine with chestnuts & smoked bacon; light casserole of rabbit with artichokes; steak & kidney pie with mashed potatoes & root vegetable purée; rack of lamb with herb crust; half a Cromer lobster. Selection of English desserts. Trad. Sun. roasts.*

The contrast in surroundings is marked enough, but here in the glorious parkland of Weston Golf Club this newish venture bears the distinctive stamp of John Brasted's other, long established restaurant, a few miles to the east in Norwich. Although naturally frequented by golfers, do not imagine that it's all Pringle sweaters and loud check trousers; this is more a restaurant with golf course attached. Parson Woodforde was a visitor to Weston House, and would feel most at home today amongst the warmth, opulence and copious food and wine - chef Adrian Ellwood trained with famous Ian McAndrew. All rooms are elegantly proportioned - superb for functions of any kind - and the tall windows afford fine views over parkland. Barbecues are held in a lovely sheltered courtyard, and a discreetly placed marquee copes with overspill.

BRASTED'S

8-10 St. Andrews Hill, Norwich Tel: (01603) 625949 Fax: (01603) 766445

Hours: Mon. - Fri. 12 to 2pm and 7 to 10pm. Sat. 7 to 10pm.
Credit cards: Mastercard, Visa, Diners, Amex.
Price guide: a la carte £24; Club Lunch £8.50, £12.50 & £16 (2,3 & 4 courses).

Examples from menus (revised seasonally): *tart of smoked haddock & leek with watercress sauce; Brasted's filo pastry cheese parcels with homemade apple & thyme jelly; quenelles of salmon in lobster sauce. Lowestoft brill in cream, mushroom & prawn sauce; braised lamb shanks with lentils; steak & kidney pudding; breasts of wild duck with Madeira & green peppercorn sauce; casserole of vegetables. Chocolate Marquise on coffee bean sauce (irresistible!); baked apple with apricots, sultanas & almonds on warm rum-scented apricot sauce; hot souffles. Savoury alternatives (a rare treat).*

John Brasted's philosophy, that one should be able to enjoy fine wines at a manageable cost, is borne out by the excellent wine list, very keenly priced for a restaurant of such high standing. The same may be said of the cooking; the Club Lunch represents outstanding value - why not make the most of it while shopping or exploring the interesting streets and alleys here in the historic city centre, by the ancient Bridewell Prison, now a museum. First take drinks in the homely morning room, then into the dining room. The welcoming, comfortable atmosphere is enhanced by draped walls and luxurious armchairs on a polished wood floor with Persian rugs, coupled with first-class service free of undue servility. Dishes featured constantly on an extensive menu include tart of fresh tomatoes, the filo pastry cheese parcels, quenelles of salmon in rich lobster sauce, and two specialities: a wonderul cassoulet and beef Stroganoff. Maximum use of fresh local produce is evident, sympathetically treated by chef Adrian Clarke.

FEMI'S RESTAURANT
42 King Street, Norwich. Tel: (01603) 766010

Hours: 12 to 2:30pm, 6:30 to 10:30pm, Tues - Sat; booking advised weekends.
Credit cards: Mastercard, Visa, Amex.
Price guide: a la carte £14.

Examples from menus (revised daily): *Norfolk pudding; cream of cauliflower & almond soup; potato & onion pancakes with smoked salmon & creme fraiche. Femi's fish ragout; poached sole fillets stuffed with crab, with rich lobster sauce; pot-roasted garlic chicken; roast loin of pork wrapped in bacon with cider brandy sauce; roast sea bass with prawn & tarragon sauce; fillet steak with wild mushrooms & madeira sauce; avocado, brie, mushrooms & fresh basil wrapped in puff pastry with red pepper sauce. Home-made desserts.*

Although not enjoying the most favourable location (tucked away behind Anglia TV), Femi's has quickly become one of the best loved restaurants in the crowded Norwich scene. It is not too hard to explain: amazingly low prices for high quality cooking. The eponymous chef proprietor trained at the London Hilton and Quaglino's - fresh fish is his speciality. Service is fast and friendly, and there are a number of nice touches: a bowl of fresh bread and jug of water on the table, petits fours to round off the meal. On three floors, the restaurant itself might be described as classical with modern touches; the authentic African decor is worth a close look. The top floor is a private dining room for up to 20.

THE AQUARIUM

22 Tombland, Norwich. Tel: (01603) 630090

Hours: 12 to 2pm, 7 to 10pm (bar open 12 to 3pm, 5 to 11pm)
daily except Suns.
Credit cards: Mastercard, Visa, Diners, Amex, Switch, Delta.
Price guide: a la carte £21; table d'hote lunch £10.50 (2 courses).

Examples from menus (revised seasonally): *Hawaiian salmon with chilli corn bread, creme fraiche & rocket; half a dozen oysters with lime wasabi dressing, avocado & spicy sausage. Roast cod fillet with ginger mash, spiced puy lentils, coriander & crispy onions; skewered monkfish with spicy black beans, guacamole, sour cream & tomato salsa; BA's killer Jamaican beef from Hell with griddled banana & sweet potato fries. Toasted chocolate & pecan loaf, battered coconut, banana & cinammon ice cream; roast strawberries, green peppercorns & vanilla ice cream.*

Norwich now has so many places to eat that to thrive each must offer something "different". This latest arrival on the scene (part of the same group as The Wildebeest Arms qv) certainly does that, not only with highly innovative food - the exotic (mostly seafood) menu draws on influences from all over the world - but also in the refreshingly new decor, which generates a unique ambience. The green velvet bar counter and matching chairs go well with black marble-effect tables; two aquaria are, unusually, vertical, and see if you can spot the upside-down jelly baby in the specially commissioned painting in the no-smoking area. One doesn't have to eat to experience all this, just have a drink in the bar - champagne happy hour is from 5pm to 7pm Monday to Friday. Terrace tables and chairs are used in good weather.

BARTON ANGLER COUNTRY INN
Irstead Road, Neatishead, nr Wroxham. Tel: (01692) 630740 Fax: (01692) 631122

Hours: 7 to 9pm daily except Mons; 12 to 3pm Suns;
bar meals lunch & evening, 7 days.
Credit cards: Mastercard, Visa, Amex.
Price guide: a la carte £20, bar meals from around £4.50.
Accommodation: 3 sngls (from £25), 4 dbls/twins (from £58); 2 with 4-posters,
all en-suite, TV, phone, tea & coff.; Oct - end of April 3 nights for price
of 2 at weekends, 4 nights for 2 midweek, with some meals incl.

Examples from menus (revised twice yearly): *hot baked crab with cream, Worcs sauce & onion, topped with cheese; beef Lord Nelson (en croute with peppers, onions & mushrooms in red wine & cream); wild boar steak flamed in Calvados; chicken supreme wrapped in bacon with brie stuffing; daily specials eg three deep-fried cheeses in Drambuie sauce, venison steak with vermouth & fresh berry sauce. Trad. Sun. roasts.* Bar: *keel pie (chicken in leek & bacon sauce); venison stew; seafood pie; cheesy courgettes; steaks; curries; lasagne. Orange & Cointreau truffle; rum roulade; apricot meringue cake.*

Not at all the usual cheap and cheerful Broadland hostelry, this handsome Regency rectory is quite unique and unashamedly select. It stands in two acres of delightful gardens, a riot of colour when the rhododendrons are in bloom - a very pleasant prospect from the restaurant, which has something of the feel of the 20s and 30s, complete with piano. With lovely Barton Broad also just across the road, not surprisingly it's a popular choice for wedding receptions - a marquee is available, and business functions are also accommodated. John and Jenwyn King have been proprietors for over 10 years; Jenwyn is a trained chef, and everything from her kitchen is fresh and home-made. Children welcome. Barbecues every Saturday evening in season.

ELDERTON LODGE HOTEL & RESTAURANT
Gunton Park, Thorpe Market. Tel: (01263) 833547 Fax: (01263) 834673

Hours: 12 to 2pm, 7 to 9pm daily; bar lunches daily.
Credit cards: Mastercard, Visa, Diners, Switch, Delta.
Price guide: set price a la carte dinner £18.50; lunch main course c. £6.
Accommodation: 11 dbls/twins; all en-suite, TV, phone, hair-dryer, tea & coff.;
£40pp per night; special breaks £55pp dinner, b & b.

Examples from menus (revised daily): *Cromer crab & coriander cakes with sweet chilli dressing; prawn & chive mousse; home-made cream of field mushroom soup. Strips of monkfish on bed of fennel, leeks & red peppers; breast of Norfolk duck with black cherry & brandy sauce; gateau of avocado, courgettes & stilton on walnut sauce. Banana pancakes with rum & butterscotch; chocolate chiffon pie. Trad. Sun. roasts plus alternatives.* Bar: *baguettes, sandwiches, many daily specials eg smoked haddock omelette with cheese sauce, mille-feuille of wok-fried chicken livers with mange tout & walnuts.*

"We won't tell anyone" say departing guests who want to keep this hidden treasure to themselves - many do come back again. But secrets will out: the major national guides have discovered this 18th-century former shooting lodge to Gunton Hall Estate, over which it commands spectacular views. Lillie Langtry entertained Edward VII here (if staying you could find yourself in her bed!), and one can see why: it is a total escape, hidden from the road in six acres of woodland, far removed from the stresses of the world. It was this and a love of Norfolk that brought Martin and Christine Worby here in March 1995. They have carefully re-invoked Edwardian elegance and have earned a good name for food, wine (tasting events are held quarterly) and a warm, personal welcome. Ideal venue for small weddings (up to 6pm) and conferences. Outdoor activities arranged. Children over six and dogs welcome.

GREEN FARM RESTAURANT & HOTEL
Thorpe Market, nr Cromer. Tel: (01263) 833602 Fax: (01263) 833163

Hours: 7 to 9pm (10pm Fri & Sat) daily; bar meals lunch & evening, 7 days).
Credit cards: Mastercard, Visa.
Price guide: a la carte £20, chef's supper £17.95; bar lunch £4.95.
Accommodation: 12 rooms; 4 with 4-posters, all en-suite, TV, tea & coff, hair-dryer
on request; £48 sngl, £70 dbl; midweek & weekend special breaks;
Tourist Board 3 Crowns commended.

Examples from menus (revised 8-10 weeks): *avocado & crab gratin; pan-fried goats' cheese with bacon & tomato salad. Lemon sorbet. Breast of chicken stuffed with banana, wrapped in bacon, with lemon butter sauce; fresh fish daily; sirloin steak with Drambuie & wild mushrooms; pasta & mushrooms baked with mozzarella & stilton. Trad. Sun roasts.* Bar: *crispy duck with orange & walnut salad; hearty casseroles; braised lamb with tomato, red wine, garlic & fresh basil. Home-made sweets.*

This classic Norfolk scene of flint cottages clustered around a village green makes an ideal escape from urban pressures. At Green Farm you will be cosseted in every creature comfort. Each individually styled bedroom is beautifully furnished; fresh flowers, fruit and home-made chocolates greet guests on arrival. The cooking is recognised as amongst the area's best; chef proprietor Philip Lomax prepares many of his own unique dishes, a delight to the eye and palate, yet at a very fair price. If you can tear yourself away there is much to see and do in these parts: Felbrigg and Blickling Hall, the Broads, Norwich and the coast are all within easy reach. Ideal venue for keen walkers and cyclists.

THE MIRABELLE
Station Road, West Runton, Cromer. Tel: (01263) 837396

Hours: open for lunch & dinner (last orders 9:15pm); closed Mons;
closed Sun. evenings in winter.
Credit cards: Mastercard, Visa, Diners, Amex.
Price guide: a la carte £17.50 - £22.50. Table d'hote £15 - £23.50. Lunch
£10.50 - £12.95. New Bistro - as many courses as you like, pub prices.
Accommodation: self-contained flat (sleeps 2) from £50 per week in winter
to £175 in summer; special all-inclusive breaks.

Examples from menus (a la carte revised seasonally, table d'hote daily): *local asparagus; Cromer crab; Hungarian goulash soup; seafood vol-au-vent; mussels. Salmon & sea bass in butter sauce; turbot; Dover sole; lobster mayonnaise/thermidor; calves liver & sweetbreads; Wienerschnitzel; game in season. Creme brulee; Viennoise apple strudel; fresh figs in Marsala; souffle glace Grand Marnier.* NEW BISTRO: *chicken Viennoise; steak & kidney pie; lemon sole meuniere; roast duckling with apple sauce; mushroom stroganoff.*

Behind a modest facade lies a large, bustling French restaurant, now in its 25th year under Austrian proprietor Manfred Hollwoger. One of the longest established and most popular in the region, it is a perennial in the national guides. Two set price menus and an a la carte add up to en extensive choice, (local seafood and game the house specialities), but now a new bistro has been added, totally informal - eat as many courses as you like, pay no more than in a pub. Even the most conventional dish is cooked and presented in a way that makes it memorable. Portions are very generous; you will not go away disappointed! Many of the wines in a truly splendid list of 350 are available by the glass. Gourmet nights in winter should not be missed - ask for a schedule. Advisable to book ahead in summer and for weekends.

THE PEPPERPOT VILLAGE RESTAURANT

Water Lane, West Runton, nr Sheringham. Tel: (01263) 837578

Hours: 12 - 2pm Tues to Sun, 7 - 10pm Tues to Sat.
Credit cards: Visa, Mastercard, Eurocard, Amex, Diners Club International.
Price guide: a la carte from £18, table d'hote £17.95; set price 3-course lunch
£10.95; Sunday lunch £11.95.

Examples from menus (revised 3-4 months): *grilled mussels in garlic sauce; melting pots of salmon & prawns; mushrooms in stilton cheese sauce. Dover sole; baked sea bass with fennel; sea trout with whole grain mustard sauce; lobster thermidor; swordfish; tournedos chasseur; venison in port & redcurrant sauce; daily home-made vegetarian dish. Lemon soufflé; cygnet surprise (meringue swan filled with fresh fruit & cream with raspberry coulis & ice cream). Choice of three Sunday roasts & supreme of salmon in white butter sauce.*

Royalty and other dignitaries have enjoyed the cooking of Ron Gattlin; during his 34 years with the RAF he was chef to Chief of Air Staff and in charge of catering at RAF Staff College, Bracknell. Now we humble civilians can also partake, here at his own beamed and chintzy restaurant quietly situated just off the main coast road, where he and wife Barbara (front of house) have earned a place in local esteem over the past seven years or so. With such depth of experience his 'repertoire' is truly comprehensive, but he does show a special flair for fresh vegetables, always interestingly presented, and for diet-busting cakes and pastries. Yet prices remain modest, even by the standards of this parsimonius region! Romantics should note in their diaries that Valentine's Supper, five courses plus nibbles to start and coffee with mints to finish, is all for just £18 currently, and no extra for the candlelight and flowers on each table!

FISHES' RESTAURANT

Market Place, Burnham Market. Tel: (01328) 738588

Hours: lunch & dinner (last orders 9:30pm, 9pm in winter)Tues - Sun. Closed over Christmas and two weeks in January.

Credit cards: Mastercard, Visa, Diners, Amex.

Price guide: a la carte £25, weekday lunch £9.40 & £11.95 (2 & 3 courses).

Examples from menus (revised seasonally): *scallop & prawns au gratin; goats' cheese with bramley & garden mint; local oysters live or baked with stilton; crab soup; melon & fresh fruit. Holkham Bay sea trout with hollandaise; halibut with garlic; salmon fishcakes with crab sauce; home-baked ham with smoked chicken. Tiramisu; sticky toffee pudding; fresh fruit salad; apple meringue 'pile-it-high' pie; home-made ice creams; fresh fruit salad. Mostly British cheeses. Children's portions.*

Burnham Market is one of Norfolk's most picturesque villages, and indeed historic: Nelson was born and raised very near here - take away the cars and he would still feel at home today. Another link with the North Sea where he learnt his craft is this perennially popular restaurant, which draws on its bounty in the form of oysters from Brancaster, crabs from Weybourne or Blakeney and much else from King's Lynn. Vegetables come fresh from local market gardeners. Featured regularly in a number of leading national good food guides, it remains nonetheless cheerfully unpretentious, bistro-style, with cork tables and floors, shelves full of books on a multitude of topics, and in summer windows full of wonderful 'Morning Glories.' Live lobsters are kept in a tank out of sight, but the cold display is tempting.

TITCHWELL MANOR HOTEL
Titchwell, nr Hunstanton. Tel: (01485) 210221 Fax: (01485) 210104

Hours: restaurant 7pm to 9:30pm daily plus Sun. lunch; bar lunchtime daily.
Credit cards: Mastercard, Visa, Diners, Amex.
Price guide: a la carte £28, table d'hote £22; bar from about £3.50 to £17.
Accommodation: 3 sngls, 11 twins/dbls, 1 family; all en-suite, TV, hair-dryer, tea & coff; 4 rooms on ground floor (good wheelchair access); special breaks throughout the year.

Examples from menus (revised daily): *chargrilled rosemary brochette of king scallops with cucumber, red onion & ginger salsa. Whole lobster on ragout of shellfish scented with chervil & saffron roquette; saddle of lamb with tomato & basil sauce set on fresh thyme; pan-fried loin of venison with confit of vegetables & port wine & tarragon jus. Jaffa cakes with Cointreau sauce; warm chocolate & fruit bread pudding. Trad. Sun. roasts.* Bar: *fish chowder; baked crab thermidor; oysters; steaks; Dover sole; sandwiches; daily specials eg fillet of grey mullet with gazpacho dressing, duckling in red wine.*

More striking inside than out, this Victorian farmhouse has been run personally by resident proprietors Margaret and Ian Snaith for over 10 years; they have built their success on personal attention and the best of fresh, mostly local produce, skilfully prepared by chefs Ben Handley and Adam Wright. The elegant lounge and dining room recapture period elegance; the latter will benefit from a new conservatory overlooking the pretty walled garden, and the newly refurbished seafood bar is bright and bistro-like, enhanced by the fabulous views across the bird reserve to the sea beyond. Bedrooms are comfortable and very good value. Small functions, children and dogs are welcome.

RISTORANTE LA VILLETTA
14 High Street, Heacham. Tel: (01485) 570928

Hours: 12 to 2pm (2:30 Suns) Tues - Sat, 7 to 10pm weekdays; 6 to10pm
Sats; closed Tuesdays in winter.
Credit cards: Mastercard, Visa.
Price guide: a la carte £18, lunch from £5; Sun lunch set price £10.95
& £11.95 (2 & 3 courses).

Examples from menu (revised seasonally): *seafood medley; mushrooms sautéed with bacon & stilton with white wine & cream sauce; vegetable pancake topped with vegetarian cheese. Monkfish flamed in Pernod with sliced mushrooms in cream sauce; breast of chicken stuffed with paté & wrapped in puff pastry, with cream sauce; escalope of veal with peppers, mushrooms, garlic & tomato sauce; nut & vegetable Wellington; pasta dishes. Italian ice creams; spotted dick; bread & butter pudding. Trad. Sun. roasts with fish alternative & full a la carte.*

The visitors' book is full of enthusiastic praise, not just for the food but also for the warm, attentive service. Carl (front of house) and Deborah (chef) Godfrey are eager to please and offer exceptional value. If you just fancy a pasta and glass of wine, that's fine, but you will be tempted by an extensive menu (including many vegetarian dishes) and wine list with a distinct Italian flavour. Guests are encouraged to linger, Italian-style; the conservatory is an ideal place in which to do so. Look out for theme nights, such as Seafood, or the very popular quarterly Ladies' Evenings (not June - Aug), a chance to socialise and see a demonstration (antiques is a favourite). The no-smoking restaurant is cool and elegant, plushly carpeted, pink and blue linen, flowers on each table, whirring ceiling fans - very suitable for a wedding reception. Watercolours by local artists for sale. Gift vouchers. Children welcome. Car park.

THE EXETER ARMS
Stamford Road, Easton-on-the-Hill, nr Stamford. Tel: (01780) 757503 Fax: (01780) 753842

Hours: 12 to 2:30pm daily, 7 to 10pm Mon - Sat.
Credit cards: Mastercard, Visa, Switch, Delta.
Price guide: a la carte dinner £17; lunch snacks from £2.75, main course from £5.50,
Sunday lunch £7.95/£10.50/£12.75 (1, 2 & 3 courses).

Examples from menus (revised seasonally): *Thai-style tiger prawns; black pudding Normande; gruyere & spinach fritters with cranberry & orange relish. Steak & kidney pudding; honey-roasted duckling with fresh rosemary & root ginger in delicate orange sauce; vegetarian specials eg spinach & chestnut roulade with plum & ginger sauce; seafood specials eg chargrilled tuna on nicoise salad, roasted fillet of sea bass. Norfolk treacle tart; chocolate & brandy terrine; fresh fruit pavlova with raspberry coulis. Lunch: fish cakes; steaks; sweet & sour chicken; Lincolnshire sausages in Yorkshire pudding; fresh pasta dishes; sandwiches. Trad. Sun. roasts plus alternatives.*

Although just outside area, an exception can be made for Easton on two grounds: it is an exquisite village, the equal of any in the Cotswolds; and, more importantly, for this very popular and honest eating house, more a restaurant than a pub. In fact it was a simple village pub from the 18th century until seven years ago, when it was transformed by chef patron David Waycot. He has built a regular clientele on the strength of fresh (never frozen!) seasonal produce (seafood a speciality) and personal attention; success has meant expansion into a new 50-seater patio garden restaurant. A marquee is also available, and with a large car park as well, this would make a fine venue for a wedding reception. It's only minutes off the A1, and very near Burleigh House, Stamford and Rutland Water.

THE BELL INN HOTEL & RESTAURANT
Great North Road, Stilton. Tel: (01733) 241066 Fax: (01733) 245173

Hours: 12 to 2pm, 7 to 9:30pm daily, bar & restaurant.
Credit cards: Visa, Mastercard, Switch.
Price guide: set price a la carte £22.50 (4 courses), table d'hote £17.95.
Accommodation: 2 sngls, 14 dbls/twins, 1 family, 2 4-posters, all en suite with
TV (incl. SKY), phone, hair-dryers, ironing boards, tea & coff.,
some with whirlpool baths; singles from £64, doubles/twins
from £79; special weekend breaks.

Examples from menus (revised weekly): *salmon & scallop timbale with tomato & coriander sauce; stilton filo baskets. Escalope of venison filled with chicken & chestnut forcemeat on cream & mushroom sauce garnished with truffle; lamb reforme; fillet of grey mullet with fine spaghetti of vegetables & crayfish sauce; mushroom & cashew nut stroganoff. Sweets from pastry kitchen; stilton & plum bread.* Bar: *Bell Inn stilton paté; king prawn & monkfish brochettte; confit of duck leg with black pudding; steak, ale & mushroom pie; pork ribs with orange & cranberry glaze. Profiteroles; lemon tart; bread & butter pudding.*

This is one of England's great (and oldest) historic coaching inns, but now that the old A1 has been by-passed it enjoys the tranquility of a country retreat. The 16th-century stonework and timbers have witnessed many a famous face: Dick Turpin, Cromwell, Lord Byron, Clark Gable and Joe Louis amongst them, not forgetting Cooper Thornhill, an 18th-century landlord who first popularised Stilton as one of the world's noblest cheeses. Modern amenities and comforts have been blended skilfully with ancient character: bedrooms are of a luxury undreamt of by earlier travellers, likewise the first class cuisine, which has won accolades from Egon Ronay and other major guides, and the ACE Hotel of the Year 1995 Award. EATB 4 Crowns Highly commended. Excellent facilities for conferences, meetings, wedding receptions etc.

BENNETT'S RESTAURANT AT THE WHITE HART
Bythorn, nr Huntingdon. Tel: (01832) 710226

Hours: restaurant 12 to 2pm, 7 to 9:30pm except Sun. evenings & Mondays;
bar bistro Tues - Sat lunch.
Credit cards: Mastercard, Visa, Switch.
Price guide: a la carte £20, bar meals c. £6.50.

Examples from menus (revised 5-weekly): *kipper pate'; potted pigeon; green herb terrine. Fillet steak & kidney pudding; salmon & scallop parcels with lobster sauce; crispy pancake stuffed with fresh vegetables & pine kernels with tomato & rosemary sauce; half roast Gressingham duck with honey, soy sauce and ginger.* Bar: *crispy loin of pork; crispy prawns in batter; game casserole; toasted brie with bacon; sirloin steak; 3-cheese ploughman's; daily specials eg spare ribs, faggots with onions. Homemade sorbets; toasted fresh fruit sabayon. Trad. Sun. roasts.*

Opened on the same day that that the old main road by which it stands was by-passed, The White Hart, more a restaurant than a pub (although drinkers are most welcome), hasn't needed passing trade. Just a mile off the new A14 in a peaceful hamlet, it draws custom from many miles around and has also not gone unnoticed by many of the major national food guides. The fact that it was once three cottages is immediately obvious on entering: stripped-wood floors, low ceilings and a truly magnificent open fireplace engender a rare sense of real atmosphere. A photo from 1910, displayed in the conservatory restaurant (which doubles for functions), shows how little things have changed. Cooking, too, is rooted in the best traditions, yet always imaginative. This food orientation extends to the reading matter thoughtfully provided by Bill Bennett in the bar. He and the cheerful staff infuse the place with a lively personality. Children welcome. Garden.

THE PHEASANT

Keyston, nr Huntingdon. Tel: (01832) 710241 Fax: (01832) 710340

Hours: 12 to 2pm, 6:30 to 10pm daily (bar & restaurant).
Credit cards: Mastercard, Visa, Diners, Amex.
Price guide: a la carte £17.50.

Examples from menus (revised fortnightly): *double-baked goats' cheese soufflé with apple & walnut salad; chicken, mushroom & basil sausage with braised lentils & vegetables; fillet of red mullet cured in honey & spices with spiced tomato & coriander sauce. Roast saddle of venison with red cabbage & celeriac purée; baked fillet of cod with herb crust & thyme sauce; char-grilled vegetables with potato & chive salad & red pepper sauce. Citrus lemon tart with creme fraiche; passion fruit delice; rich chocolate marquis with coffee sauce. Trad. Sun. roasts.*

Revered locally and praised by all the main national guides, this picturesque 17th century thatched inn is a classic of its kind, replete with old timbers and log fires, and overlooking a textbook village green. But a glance at the menu above will confirm this is much more a sophisticated restaurant than a country pub (although drinkers are made welcome). It is as relaxed as any pub, however, in keeping with its stablemates, the Three Horseshoes at Madingley, Old Bridge Hotel in Huntingdon and White Hart, Gt Yeldham. Like them it also boasts an outstanding wine list. Chef patron is Martin Lee, who previously worked at the celebrated Le Manoir Aux Quat' Saisons and with Paul Heathcote. Functions up to 30 in restaurant.

OLD BRIDGE HOTEL

1 High Street, Huntingdon. Tel: (01480) 452681 Fax: (01480) 411017

Hours: 12 to 2:30pm,
6 to 10:30pm daily
(bar & restaurant).
Credit cards: Mastercard, Visa,
Diners, Amex.
Price guide: a la carte £18.
Accommodation: 7 sngls, 19 dbls/twins
all en suite, satellite
TV, hair dryer, trouser
press,complimentary
newspaper; rooms
from £67.50 to £120
per night; special
weekend breaks
£67.50 (dinner, b & b).

Examples from menus (revised monthly): *smooth chicken liver paté with onion marmalade & toast; salad of rocket, courgette, Japanese cress, basil, parmesan & pine kernels. Grilled mackerel with butterbean, tomato & mustard casserole & grilled ciabatta bread; rack of spring lamb with courgette, tomato, mint & tabbouleh (cold spiced cous cous). Panacotta (vanilla cream) with compote of strawberries; chocolate nemesis with creme fraiche. Lunchtime buffet Mon - Fri. Sunday lunch: roast sirloin of beef.*

One of the most respected and best known in the county, this elegant 18th-century hotel (the flagship of the Huntsbridge Group of The Pheasant, Keyston, Three Horseshoes, Madingley and White Hart, Gt Yeldham) is also one of the most opulent. Richly decorated throughout with the finest fabrics (and the bathrooms are luxurious!), it remains nonetheless remarkably 'unstarchy'. The staff are cheerful and courteous, and one may eat what and where one likes. Chef patron Nick Steiger is experienced in top establishments in London and Oxford, while Managing Director John Hoskins is the industry's only "Master of Wine" and winner of Egon Ronay's "Cellar of the Year" for the best wine list in the UK (many available by the glass). The restaurant is clearly no mere appendage, and rates in just about every leading national guide. The hotel is well situated for an overnight stay, on the banks of the River Ouse and just a short stride from the shops. Cambridge and Grafham water are easily reached. Function room for 30. Live jazz on the terrace first Friday of each month

THE PLATE & PORTER

210 Station Road, March. Tel. & Fax: (01354) 660322

Hours: 12 to 2pm Tues - Sun; 7 to 9pm Tues - Sat.
Credit cards: Mastercard, Visa, Diners, Switch, Delta.
Price guide: a la carte £16.

Examples from menus (revised every 5-6 months): *Thai crab cakes on bed of bean sprouts with red curry & coconut sauce; terrine of duck & pork with spicy pear chutney; selection of mixed mushrooms in white wine & herb sauce in pastry case. Sea bream with zingy couscous & red pepper essence; fillet of Scotch beef layered between mushroom ragout on red wine & truffle sauce; pan-fried breast of chicken glazed with almonds on plum & honey sauce; pasta dishes; seasonal specials. Soft chocolate cake with mascarpone sorbet; exotic fresh fruit salad in brandysnap basket with duo of sauces; banana creme brulée.*

Fenland has been a 'graveyard' for many a hopeful new restaurateur, but here is a notable exception. Family-owned and run since Nov. '95, this Victorian former hotel (next to the station) has become very popular indeed, especially busy on Saturday evenings (so book well ahead), drawing custom from many miles around. Outstanding value is surely the keystone - the chef proprietor has worked in top London restaurants which would charge three or four times as much for cooking of this quality - coupled with a good atmosphere. The main dining room is light and airy, with pastel pink walls, cream linen, flowers and prints. There is a pleasant second dining room available for small functions. Can you deduce how the restaurant got its name?

THE FEN HOUSE RESTAURANT
2 Lynn Road, Littleport, nr Ely. Tel: (01353) 860645

The Fen House
Restaurant

Hours: 7 to 9pm (last orders), Wed - Sat; lunches by arrangement.
Credit cards: Mastercard, Visa.
Price guide: set price a la carte £26 (4 courses).

Examples from menus (revised monthly): *lightly cooked fillets of wild rabbit flavoured with cinnamon & Sauternes, served on potato cakes with apple; salad of smoked eel with basil & creme fraiche; asparagus soup with wild mushrooms. Fillet of brill with olive topping & caper sauce; roasted saddle of lamb with mustard noodles & light seed mustard sauce; crispy vegetables in pastry case with tangy coriander sauce. Caramelised roasted pears with honey ice cream; rich chocolate mousse sandwiched between crisp chocolate layers surrounded by raspberry sauce.*

Michelin and other acknowledged arbiters of good taste laud this little 22-seater gem, heartily endorsed by a well established clientele. David and Gaynor Warne have worked hard over 11 years to earn this recognition for their comfortable, elegant 17th-century cottage out in the 'wilds' of Fenland. One may arrive by car, boat or train (the river and station are very near), and can always look forward to a warm reception from Gaynor, and a well considered and balanced menu prepared by David himself (formerly of The Savoy and Buckingham Palace), to be savoured in relaxed surroundings. All is fresh and home-made, even bread and ice cream. 50 or so wines appear on a very good, reasonably priced list. Ask to go on the waiting list for membership of the LUNCHEON CLUB (£10 fee); it's very friendly, with lively discussion over a three-course meal and wine.

THE ANCHOR INN

Sutton Gault, Sutton, nr Ely. Tel: (01353) 778537 Fax: (013~~~

CAMBRIDGESH.

Hours: 12 to 2pm, 7 to 9pm daily.
Credit cards: Mastercard, Visa, Switch, Delta, Amex.
Price guide: a la carte £22, set-price lunch £14.95 (3 courses),
lunchtime specials from £5.
Accommodation: 2 dbls/twins, both en suite, sitting room, TV, phone,
dryer, tea & coff; TB 3 Crowns Highly Commended,
AA QQQQ; from £55 per room; special 3-night winter breaks.

Examples from menus (revised daily): *grilled dates wrapped in bacon on a mild mustard sauce; herring fillets in Madeira marinade. Fresh fillet of salmon with watercress cream; wild rabbit braised in cider with bacon, mustard, prunes & herbs; steak, kidney & Guinness pie; mushroom, herb, red wine & blue cheese pancake. Passion fruit creme brulée with home-made vanilla biscuit; chocolate Bavarian cream with apricot sauce. Good selection of cheeses.* Bar *(lunchtime only): own-recipe sausages in red wine with garlic mash; wild mushroom omelette; potted duck with crusty bread. Trad. Sun. roasts.*

Les Routiers Inn of the Year; Cambridge Dining Pub of the Year from another major guide; a Rosette from the Consumer's Association; featured on local TV: despite its glorious solitude, this remarkably preserved (the bar is still gaslit) 350-year-old riverside ferry inn is well and truly 'on the map', even if Sutton Gault itself is not (turn off the B1381 just south of Sutton village). Credit is due to proprietor Robin Moore, assisted by chef Mark Corcoran; their ever-changing menus are supplemented by monthly Gourmet Nights on Tuesdays in winter, and there's occasional wine tasting (ask to go on mailing list). Spectacular sunsets and views from bedroom windows. Small function room.

71

THE THREE HORSESHOES

Madingley, nr Cambridge. Tel: (01954) 210221 Fax: (01954) 212043

Hours: 12 to 2pm, 6:30 to 10pm daily (bar & restaurant).
Credit cards: Mastercard, Visa, Diners, Amex.
Price guide: a la carte £18.

Examples from menus (revised three-weekly): *chargrilled scallops with wilted raddicio, chard & chicory, with 30-year-old balsamic vinegar & chive oil; Tuscan bread soup with tomato, beans, cabbage & olive oil. Grilled skate wing with butter beans, rosemary, spinach & lemon butter; pan-fried duck with duck confit, champ, greencabbage, bacon & lentils with red wine & thyme; twice-baked aubergine & ricotta soufflé; roast haunch of venison with red onion marmalade, fondant potato, leeks, mushrooms & juniper. Sunday lunch: roast sirloin of beef.*

Cambridge is surely the region's most visited city, and the consequent bustle can be quite taxing. But just two miles away is to be found this idyllic retreat, a 17th-century thatched inn surrounded by parkland. Highly rated by nearly all the major national good food and pub guides, it is best described as a quality restaurant, although guests are most welcome to just call in for a drink in the bar. One may dine in the bar or the elegant conservatory overlooking the large garden. Richard Stokes is the chef patron, having trained at the famous George Hotel, Stamford and Flitwick Manor. Managing Director is John Hoskins, a wine expert of national standing, whose aim is to list the 100 most interesting wines to be found. Egon Ronay and the Good Food Guide have judged the choice to be outstanding. The Three Horseshoes flourishes as part of the prestigious quartet which includes the Old Bridge Hotel at Huntingdon, The Pheasant at Keyston and White Hart, Gt Yeldham, and follows the same philosophy of friendly informality.

DUXFORD LODGE HOTEL
& LE PARADIS RESTAURANT
Ickleton Road, Duxford. Tel: (01223) 836444 Fax: (01223) 832271

Hours: 12 to 2pm, 7 to 9:30pm, daily except Sat. lunch.
Credit cards: Mastercard, Visa, Diners, Amex, Switch, Delta.
Price guide: a la carte £24, table d'hote lunch & dinner £18.50;
business lunch £10.95; trad. Sun. roasts £14.95
Accommodation: 2 sngls, 13 dbls, 1 twin, 2 family; 2 with 4-posters, some with sofas,
1 air-conditioned; all en-suite, TV, phone, hair-dryer, trouser press,
tea   & coff., large baths; from £40 sngl, £75 dbl at weekends
(subject to availability); from £70 sngl, £90 dbl, £95
Executive rooms weekdays.

Examples from menus (a la carte revised seasonally, table d'hote daily): *deep-fried crab & prawn croquettes with mango & coriander salsa; baked breast of quail in filo pastry with truffle & mushroom duxelle & light Madeira jus. Baked breast of chicken filled with fresh crab meat flavoured with ginger & sherry; tenderloin of pork inter-leaved with honeyed sweet pepper & onion confit & cumin spiced cream; vegetarian dish of the day. Creme de Menthe brulée topped with white & dark chocolate copeaux; capuccino & rum truffle cup with Bacardi & vanilla custard.*

One of very few establishments in the county to be awarded the RAC Blue Ribbon and AA Two Rosettes, this handsome turn-of-the century country house is a tranquil retreat just off the M11, owned and run for six years by Ron and Sue Craddock (formerly of the Saffron Hotel, Saff. Walden). The air-conditioned restaurant is a particularly pleas-ant room, decorated with paintings of exotic birds and overlooking the lovely one-acre garden and sun terrace - wonderful venue for a wedding reception (there's also a private restaurant and good conference facilities). English, French and Italian chefs make for a cosmopolitan kitchen which enjoys an excellent reputation.

THE PINK GERANIUM

Station Road, Melbourn, nr Royston (Herts). Tel: (01763) 260215 Fax: (01763) 262110

Hours: open for lunch & dinner Mon - Fri, Sat lunch private parties,
Sat dinner, plus Sunday lunch.
Credit cards: Mastercard, Switch, Visa, Amex.
Price guide: a la carte £35 - £40; Contemporary Luncheon Menu 2 courses £12;
Contemporary Evening Menu (not Sat) 2 courses £20; Contemporary Sat
Evening Menu 3 courses £30; Sunday Luncheon 3 courses £22.50.

Examples from menus (revised seasonally): *Confit of pork & foie gras; Crostini of wood pigeon; Chargrilled tuna with crispy aubergine. Roasted sea bass; Cannon of wild venison; Duckling with its own confit; Fillet of beef with rösti & wild mushrooms. Assiette of desserts. Freshly ground coffee & truffles.*

The Pink Geranium is a beautiful thatched cottage (circa 1500) set in a traditional English garden. Proprietors Sally and Steven Saunders run the restaurant to the highest of standards. It is listed in all major food guides and has a national following since Steven became a regular chef on television with 'Ready Steady Cook' and numerous other daytime cookery shows. Head chef Mark Jordan (ex 'Four Seasons', London) maintains the prestige and culinary expertise that everyone has come to expect. A la carte prices reflect the use of premium quality ingredients; daily contemporary menus are remarkably reasonably priced, and show great integrity and skill. Booking essential. Civil wedding licence, outside catering for up to 200. Private function room/conference facilities. Steven's "Hands On" Cookery School (day and monthly rates) is very popular - for details and brochure call Julie Seymour on (01763) 260215

NICHOLL'S BRASSERIE

38 The Embankment, Bedford. Tel: (01234) 212848 Fax: (01234) 212847

Hours: 10am to 10pm Mon - Sat, Sun Brunch from 10am onwards.
Credit cards: Mastercard, Visa, Amex.
Price guide: a la carte £13-16.

Examples from menus (revised 3 times p.a.): *warm salmon tart with asparagus salad & dill & lemon dressing; crispy duck leg with sesame plum sauce on cucumber & green onion salad; plum tomatoes with peppered salami, foccacia & rocket salad. Nicholl's own fishcakes; guinea fowl with cider & mustard sauce; spaghetti with mushrooms, roast peppers, tomatoes & boursin cheese; daily specials eg prawn & swordfish brochette with sweet & sour sauce. Cambridge burnt cream; toffee apple crumble; glazed pineapple with coconut ice cream & apricot sauce. Trad. Sun. roasts.*

The provincial English brasserie, serving good food all day at affordable prices, is enjoying phenomenal growth. The Nicholl's chain has opened four in rapid succession, the other three being: Woburn (qv); Adelaide Street, St Albans (tel: 01727 811889); 163-165 High St Berkhamsted (tel: 01442 879988). The menu is the same at each, though blackboard specials differ, but quality and consistency are the foundation stones. 10-15 minutes' walk from the shops, in Bedford's smartest quarter, facing the river (boats for hire) and adjacent to a garden park (open air theatre planned), this dignified Edwardian building is well suited for the house style of polished wood floors, Bentwood furniture, mirrors and plants; sitting out on the front patio, overlooking the River Ouse, is a delight. Trad. jazz trio every other Sunday.

THE KNIFE & CLEAVER

Houghton Conquest, nr Bedford. Tel: (01234) 740387 Fax: (01234) 740900

Hours: 12 to 2:30pm, 7 to 9:30pm daily except Sun. evenings.
Credit cards: Mastercard, Visa, Diners, Amex.
Price guide: a la carte £22; table d'hote £18.50 (3 courses); lunch £11.95
(2 courses), Sun lunch £13.50 (3 courses).
Accommodation: 9 dbls/twins (3 de luxe, 6 stndrd); all en-suite, TV, phone, fridge,
hair dryer, tea & coff. RAC & AA 2*; from £45 sngl,
£59 dbl; dbl at sngl rate weekends.

Examples from menus (revised monthly): *pan-fried crab & salmon cakes with pineapple salsa & lime creme fraiche; special pigeon terrine. Fresh fish specials eg roasted darne of sea bass with scallops & pomme elli & morel mushroom jus; three-spiced fillet steak on mascarpone risotto rice; pasta ragout of fresh asparagus, artichoke hearts and melted mozzarella. Terrine of gooseberry ice cream & gingerbread with vanilla creme fraiche; brioche & butter pudding with rum.* Bar: *garlicky Toulouse sausages with mashed potatoes & onion gravy; crabmeat burger in toasted muffin; home-made foccacia bread sandwich with whole chicken breast, bacon & tomato. Trad. Sun. roasts.*

This is one of the county's most widely respected restaurants (recently chosen to cater for the Queen and recipient of AA Rosette), established as such over eight years by David and Pauline Loom, and one of the few where truly fresh fish (a speciality) may be enjoyed. The air-conditioned conservatory dining room (available for functions) is light and airy, and overlooks the flower-bedecked terrace. If eating informally, the bar is also very pleasant, with oak panelling (from nearby Houghton House), low beams and a feature fireplace. Every six weeks on a Friday is a special evening, eg Midsummer live jazz; or try a wine evening, such as Bordeaux, with food to match (ask to go on the mailing list). Spoil yourself with an overnight stay and relax over the papers and a hearty breakfast.

NICHOLL'S BRASSERIE
13 Bedford Street, Woburn. Tel: (01525) 290896 Fax: (01525) 290596

Hours: 11am to 2:30pm, 6:30 to 10pm Mon - Sat; Sun Brunch
from 10:30am onwards.
Credit cards: Mastercard, Visa.
Price guide: a la carte £13-16.

Examples from menus (revised 3 times p.a.): *grilled Mediterranean prawns with garlic butter; onion bread bruschetta with marinaded peppers, tomato juice & parmesan shavings; creamed smoked trout with toasted country bread. Baked cod with basil, courgettes & seafood bisque; spicy falafels with aubergine ragout & cucumber & yoghurt sauce; braised leg of lamb with coriander, curry spices & basmati rice; daily specials eg cajun spiced smoked salmon with salsa verde & green salad. Summer pudding with lavender ice cream; spiced pears poached in red wine; warm chocolate fudge cake. Trad. Sun. roasts.*

"A come-and-come again place" - the thinking behind the four new Nicholl's Brasseries, the other three being at Bedford (qv); 163-165 High St, Berkhamsted (tel: 01442 879988); Adelaide Street, St Albans (tel: 01727 811889). The menu is the same at each, save for the daily specials, and so is the recipe of quality and consistency at exceptionally fair prices. Also good value, the wine list has been selected to match the cuisine. One of England's most stately and historic villages (with a lot of antique shops!), Woburn is the perfect setting for the classic provincial brasserie - warm gold walls, polished wood floors, Bentwood furniture, mirrors and plants, in a Georgian building. Trad. jazz trio every other Sunday. Woburn Abbey nearby. Ample parking.

ANNIE'S BISTRO
2 Leighton Street, Woburn. Tel: (01525) 290300

Hours: Tues 12 to 3pm; Wed & Thurs 11am to 6pm; Fri 11am to 5pm & 7pm
to 9:30pm; Sat 10am to 5pm & 7pm to 9:30pm;
Sun 10am to 6pm. Closed Mons.
Credit cards: Mastercard, Visa, Delta, Switch.
Price guide: set price dinner £14.95 & £17.95 (2 & 3 courses); lunch from £1.95.

Examples from dinner menus (revised fortnightly): *wild boar rillaud with onion bread; smoked salmon ravioli in fine herb sauce & toasted pecoroni cheese. Chicken, broccoli & mushroom crumble with saffron sauce; grilled fillet of sole on bed of creamed spinach with tarragon cream sauce; pan-fried sirloin with brie, caramelised apples & calvados. White chocolate & peanut torte; chilled ginger wine soufflé; strawberry pavlova with clotted cream.* Lunch: *poached egg on muffins with curried prawns; spicy sausages with creamed potatoes & onion gravy; seafood crepes with blue cheese & parsley sauce; cauliflower cheese with crispy bacon or toasted cashews; lightly spiced fish soup. Banana pavlova with butterscotch sauce; chilled orange pudding. Trad. Sun. roasts. ALSO: all-day breakfasts; morning coffee; afternoon teas (home-made cakes, scones, muffins); outside catering.*

Immensely popular locally, and a favourite of the many visitors to this, one of England's finest towns (a Mecca for antique-hunters), Annie's somehow successfully wears at least three hats - a high class tea room, lunchtime bistro and, on Friday and Saturday evenings, a serious quality restaurant - all offering remarkably good value. Unbelievably there is only ever one chef in the kitchen: Andy Bone or Dale Kilby (proprietors). The table is yours for the evening and will not be too close to the next one; with soft pink walls, wood half-panelling and cottagey furnishings, it's all very relaxing and agreeable. Good, inexpensive wine list. Limited edition prints for sale. Tables and chairs outside. Easy parking.

JUST 32
32 Sun Street, Hitchin. Tel: (01462) 455666

Hours: 12 to 2:30pm, 7 to 10pm Mon - Fri; 6 to 10:30pm Sats.
Credit cards: Mastercard, Visa, Amex, Diners, Switch, Delta, Electron, Solo, JCB.
Price guide: a la carte £22.50 (for 3 courses, set price per course).

Examples from menus (revised monthly): *salmon & corn cakes with tomato & basil salsa & lemon aioli; baked tomato with goats' cheese, asparagus, basil & garlic; salad of red roast pork with seared scallops & Thai dressing. Fillet of Scotch beef with wasabi mash, stir-fried paksoi & five-spice gravy; maple-roast chicken breast with salad of roasted provencale vegetables; grilled polenta with roasted tomatoes, roasted asparagus & gorgonzola; blackboard fish specials eg roast hake (with chargrilled peppers, bacon, olive oil, mash & meat gravy). Chocolate truffle cake; hot French apple tart with caramel sauce; poached pear with blue cheese.*

Just 32 yards or so off Hitchin's pleasantly continental-style town square, here is a much needed new entry to the Hertfordshire scene. Run by talented chef Robert Armstrong, it is owned by David and Pauline Loom, who have made the Knife and Cleaver at Houghton Conquest (qv) one of the very best restaurants in Bedfordshire. Like its sister restaurant, Just 32 has a penchant for fresh seafood, bought in daily according to market, and prepared in highly original ways. Also very different are the special events, like Celebration of Spring or Oscar Wilde Night; a classical guitarist is planned. Nearly all wines are available by the glass or in carafes. The pleasing interior is much older (16th-century) and more characterful than would appear from the out-side, with timber beams, stripped wood floor and a very sloping ceiling! Easy parking on the streets in the evening, or public car park nearby.

REDCOATS FARMHOUSE HOTEL

Redcoats Green, nr Hitchin. Tel: (01438) 729500 Fax: (01438) 723322
Mail: redcoatsfarmhouse@ukbusiness.com URL: http://www.infotel.co.uk.17368

Hours: 12 to 1:30pm (daily except Sats), 7 to 9pm (daily except Suns). Closed Bank Hols.
Credit cards: Mastercard, Visa, Diners, Amex.
Price guide: a la carte £30; Club Lunch £14 & £16 (2 & 3 courses); Supper Menu from £3.50; Sun. lunch £16.
Accommodation: 1 sngl, 13 dbls/twins; 12 en suite, TV, phone, hair dryer, tea & coff; from £75 sngl, £85 dbl, weekend breaks from £100 for 2 nights dinner, b & b.

Examples from menus (revised fortnightly): *fresh scampi tails in garlic butter; home-made rabbit brawn with mustard pickle; roasted tomato salad with pinenuts & olives. Fresh hake cutlet au poivre; fillet steak topped with Guinness & cheddar; grouse served with fried breadrumbs & whisky gravy; casserole of mixed vegetables & pulses on wild rice. Home-made Toblerone & sherry ice cream; peach pudding with walnut & butterscotch sauce; savouries eg angels on horseback,Welsh rarebit. Trad. Sun. roasts.*

"Not so much an hotel, more a way of life" say Peter Butterfield and sister Jackie Gainsford. This 15th-century farmhouse has been in their family since 1916, and is homely in the way that only a family-run business can be, with antiques and paintings, open fireplaces, exposed timbers and an attractive conservatory overlooking the 4-acre garden - a lovely location for a wedding (licensed for civil ceremonies, and marquee available). Tellingly, chef John Ruffle has worked here for over 17 years, and has earned consistent ratings in the major good food and hotel guides. Customers become devotees - most of the business is repeat bookings. Tranquil and unspoilt, Redcoats Green is only minutes from the A1 and 35 miles from central London, yet not on the maps - find it off the A602 towards Little Wymondley.

▲▼

RECIPES

▲▼

CRISPY CHEESE BEIGNETS
(from Hedgehogs, Kelsale)

INGREDIENTS (16 QUENELLES - SERVES 4)

0.5 pint water

4ozs butter

5ozs strong plain flour

8ozs mixed grated cheese
eg gruyere, cheddar

3 - 4 eggs

fresh chives, chopped

salt & pepper

METHOD

Bring water, butter, salt & pepper to boil
Take off heat
Stir in flour, return to heat, stirring for 1 min.
Place in mixer and beat, slowly adding eggs until dropping consistency is achieved
Slowly add cheeses & chives
Shape into quenelles
Deep-fry at 160-170°c until floating and golden brown

Serve hot with pre-prepared tomato, olive & basil salad

BERMUDA FISH CHOWDER
(from Scott's Brasserie, Ipswich)

INGREDIENTS

1kg fish fillet, cubed 3 bay leaves

3 ltrs fish stock 4 cloves

1 large leek 1 tbsp tomato paste

3 medium carrots ½ tsp chilli powder

1 head celery ½ tsp cinnamon

1 large onion 2 dashes Worcs sauce

3 large tomatoes, blanched

2 dashes tabasco

2 cloves garlic salt & pepper to taste

1 tbsp thyme flour & water

1 tbsp marjoram gravy browning

1 tbsp oregano dark rum & sherry
peppers

METHOD
Sweat off the vegetables
Add fish stock
Add all herbs & spices
Bring to the boil and simmer for 20 mins
Add fish fillet and simmer for 10 mins
Mix flour & water to a thick paste
Add flour to thicken soup
Add splash of gravy browning for richer colour
Check seasoning
Simmer for a further 30 mins
Serve with a splash of dark rum & sherry peppers, chunky bread

TIGER PRAWNS PAN-FRIED WITH TOMATO & BASIL PISTOU

(from Riverside Restaurant, Woodbridge)

INGREDIENTS (SERVES 4)

20 tiger prawns, shelled and raw

5 large beef tomatoes

4 shallots, peeled and finely chopped

1 bunch fresh basil, shredded

3 tbsp olive oil

pinch ground coriander

METHOD

Blanch tomatoes in boiling water for 10 seconds
Refresh in iced water until completely cold
Drain and remove skins
Cut into quarters and de-seed
Bind together tomatoes, shallots and basil with three tbsp olive oil and pinch of coriander
Gently heat in frying pan 1 tbsp of olive oil and add tiger prawns
Fry for two mins on each side and gently add tomato mixture
Divide into four serving dishes with some freshly cooked egg pasta

SMOKED SCALLOPS WITH SPINACH & ITALIAN BACON
(from Little Hammonds Restaurant, Ingatestone)

INGREDIENTS

4 large scallops

2 slices bacon

4ozs spinach

garnish

seasoning

METHOD

Sauté spinach in butter, keep warm
Smoke scallops in smoking tin for 3 mins
Finish by frying scallops and put on top of spinach
Garnish with pancetta roasted Italian bacon

Sauce:
0.5 pint of veal stock reduced
Add 2ozs red wine, reduce
Add 2ozs cream, reduce
Season, add around the scallops

HOME-CURED SALMON FILLET
(from Ye Olde Honingham Buck, Honingham)

INGREDIENTS

4.5lb salmon fillet, skinned & boned

6 cloves garlic, thinly sliced

2 tbsp pink peppercorns

12 turns on a pepper mill

juice & zest of 1 lime

juice & zest of 2 lemons

8 fl ozs walnut oil

1 tsp sea salt

1oz grated fresh ginger

4 tsp thyme leaves

2tsp dil leaves

shake of balsamic vinegar

half glass dry white wine

METHOD

Mix all ingredients together in a bowl

Take a piece of foil larger than the salmon and spread half the mixture on the foil, then place salmon on the mix

Turn up edges of foil to prevent juices escaping

Spread remaining mix over the salmon

Wrap tightly in the foil and place in fridge

Turn twice daily, putting back any juices which may have seeped

After 4 days salmon will be 'cured' - may be eaten cold (thinly sliced) or hot, cut into 0.75" slices (simply pan-fry for approx. one minute either side and serve on bed of warm new potato salad).

SALAD OF CRAB, AVOCADO &
APPLE WITH SAMPHIRE &
A TOMATO VINAIGRETTE
(from Old Bridge Hotel, Huntingdon)

INGREDIENTS

fresh crab or crab meat (cooked)

little mayonnaise

seasoning

apple, finely diced

avocado finely diced

little squeeze of lemon juice

Tomato vinaigrette:

2oog ripe tomato

10ml good olive oil

1tsp sugar

juice of 1 lemon

samphire, washed & lightly dressed with
good vinaigrette

METHOD

Mix white crab meat with brown in ratio 4:1
Bind this with mayonnaise and adjust seasoning
At last minute mix in apple, avocado & squeeze of lemon juice
Set this mix on middle of plate, using a cutting ring to form a smooth circle
Top with a nice selection of salads, sparingly dressed

Place ripe tomatoes in liquidiser, along with olive oil, sugar and lemon juice
"Blitz" the mix then strain through a conical strainer
Drizzle a little of this around the crab
Garnish with sprigs of samphire

LOIN OF WILD HARE WITH HOT BEETROOT SAUCE
(from Whitehall Hotel, Broxted)

INGREDIENTS

Two 8oz loins of wild hare (weight off the bone)

4 rashers smoked back bacon

4oz grated apple

4oz grated celeriac

4oz grated potato

4oz fine stripped beetroot

½ onion, finely sliced

4oz button mushrooms, sliced

1 glass Madeira

½ glass brandy

1 pint beef stock

4 sprigs flat parsley leaf

METHOD

Wrap boneless hare loins in the bacon
Slowly cook onions in a little butter until soft
Add sliced mushrooms and cook until they are soft
Add brandy, set alight and reduce liquid by half
Add Madeira and reduce liquid by half again
Add beef stock and reduce liquid by half
Pass sauce through a fine sieve, season to taste and keep warm
Mix all the grated ingredients together and season
Heat a small frying pan, add some oil and when hot add grated ingredients - try to keep in round, flat shape
When golden brown on one side turn and cook other side to same colour - keep hot
Roast wild hare at 200°c for about 20 mins. When cooked leave to rest a few mins
Return sauce to heat, add beetroot
Place grated rosti in middle of plate
Slice hare and arrange in fan on top of rosti
Pour over sauce and garnish with flat-leaf parsley

CHAR-GRILLED MEDALLIONS OF GUNTON PARK VENISON WITH HEDGEROW BLACKBERRIES & AN ELDERBERRY JUS

(from Elderton Lodge Hotel & Restaurant, Thorpe Market)

INGREDIENTS

Fillet of venison - 6ozs per portion

0.5lb fresh blackberries

2 tsp honey

0.5lb elderberries

0.5 pint venison stock

1 onion, diced

1 glass red wine

salt & mill pepper

METHOD

Bring blackberries, honey & red wine to boil, switch off
Sweat the onion in a little vegetable oil
Add elderberries & stock, boil for 2 - 3 mins
Liquidize

Lightly char-grill the medallions of venison for 2-3 mins each side
Place three piles of blackberries around the plate
Put medallions in the centre, pour jus over
Garnish with bunches of fresh elderberries

Season to taste

HALF PHEASANT BRAISED WITH SWEET VERMOUTH & BLACK GRAPES
(from Prince of Wales, Broxted)

INGREDIENTS (SERVES 6)

half pint sweet vermouth

3 pheasants (halved)

half pound black seedless grapes

1 medium onion, sliced

1 tsp fresh thyme

1.5 pints beef stock

METHOD

Place roasting tray over a medium flame with a little vegetable oil
Fry onion until soft
Add grapes and stir-fry for a further 2 mins
Remove from heat and put onion & grapes to one side
Return tray to heat
Lay pheasant skin-side down and brown for 3 or 4 mins
Turn pheasants over and repeat
Spoon grape & onion mixture over the pheasant
Sprinkle thyme over the top
Add vermouth to the tray
Bring to boil, reduce by half
Add beef stock and season
Cover with foil and braise on Gas Mark 6 for 2 hours
When cooked, thicken sauce with a little cornflour
Add cold water in a saucepan

As a final touch you may like to garnish with crispy croutons

BREAST OF DUCK DIJONNAISE
(from Mill Inn, Market Weston)

INGREDIENTS (FOR 2)

2 duck breasts (seasoned)

oil for frying (sunflower)

salt & pepper

Sauce:

4ozs blackcurrants

2 tsp sugar

zest & juice of 1 orange

1 tbsp cassis

0.25 pint chicken stock (cold)

1.5 tsp cornflour

METHOD

Heat oil in frying pan and brown duck breasts on both sides
Reduce heat, cover and cook slowly for 10-15 mins until just pink in the middle
Put onto a plate and keep warm
Put stock and cornflour into pan with meat juices and bring to boil, stirring until
thickened
Strain into clean saucepan
Put blackcurrants & sugar into a saucepan, cook slowly to a purée and sieve into stock
Add cassis, zest & juice of orange and simmer for 2 mins
Cut duck breasts on the slant, arrange on a plate and partially mask with the sauce
Serve with new potatoes & selection of fresh vegetables

CHICKEN BREASTS WITH SHERRY & TARRAGON
(from The Angel Hotel, Lavenham)

INGREDIENTS (SERVES 4)

4 chicken breasts

1 medium onion, finely chopped

little butter

1 large glass medium sherry

chicken stock

few sprigs fresh tarragon

button mushrooms, sliced

good dollop of double cream

little cornflour

seasoning

METHOD

In a large saucepan cook onion in butter until soft
Meanwhile brown chicken breasts on both sides in butter in frying pan over medium heat
Add chicken breasts to saucepan of onions in one layer if possible
Deglaze frying pan with sherry
Add sherry to saucepan containing onions and breasts
Add enough chicken stock to cover breasts
Tuck sprigs of tarragon around chicken breasts
Cover pan and simmer gently until breasts are cooked through
Remove chicken breasts and keep warm
Add mushrooms and cream, boil to reduce and thicken - add cornflour if necessary
Adjust seasoning to taste
Return chicken breasts to pan before serving

CHICKEN, WILD MUSHROOM & BASIL SAUSAGE WITH BRAISED LENTILS
(from Pheasant, Keyston)

INGREDIENTS

Chicken sausage:

300g chicken breast

200g minced chicken leg meat

400ml cream

200g assorted wild mushrooms

30g fresh basil

Braised lentils:

150g lentils du puy

3 medium carrots

2 medium courgettes

1 medium onion

bunch fresh tarragon

1 clove garlic

meat stock (pref. veal or brown chicken)

METHOD
Sausage:
Roughly dice chicken breast & purée in processor (don't overheat)
Add half the cream and liquidize a few more seconds
Wash and trim mushrooms; sauté in a little unsalted butter, season, leave to cool
Finely chop basil; fold all ingredients together with minced leg and remainder of cream
Test mixture by placing small amount on a piece of clingfilm; wrap tightly and place in a
pan of simmering water for 3 mins; remove and test for seasoning
Roll all the mixture with clingfilm into sausages approx. 4-5" long
Blanch for 8 - 10 mins, then refresh in cold water
Refrigerate until needed

Lentils:
Dice carrots, courgettes, onions & garlic; sauté in unsalted butter until tender
Put lentils in cold water, season and bring to boil
When boiled strain water and re-boil with fresh water
Cook until tender
When cooked refresh in cold water, then drain
Add lentils to diced vegetables
Add meat stock & chopped tarragon, simmer for 10 mins
To serve, unwrap sausages and brown in frying pan, then roast in oven for 3-4 mins
Serve on bed of heated lentils with a little stock

SAUTÉ OF CHICKEN LIVERS IN MADEIRA & CREAM

(from William Bavin of Weavers, Diss)

INGREDIENTS (PER PERSON)

3ozs chicken livers

1 tbsp medium Madeira

2 tbsp double cream

salt & pepper

½oz butter

1 slice toasting bread

METHOD

Trim livers, removing any sinuous fat
Cut to equal squares
Melt butter in sauté pan
Seal livers and season
Add Madeira
Add double cream and reduce to a syrup
Serve immediately onto hot toast and garnish with small dressed salad.

NB: do not allow livers to overcook; they should be spongy and pink inside.

PEPPERED LAMBS' KIDNEYS & MUSHROOMS
(from Kevin Ellis, head chef at The Cricketers, Reydon)

INGREDIENTS

1.5lb lambs' kidneys

12ozs button mushrooms, finely chopped and quartered

1 medium onion, chopped

1 glass sherry

0.75 pint double cream

2ozs butter

freshly milled black pepper

METHOD

Prepare kidneys by cutting in half and cutting out sinew

Heat sauté pan - add butter

When hot, add onions - sauté until transparent

Add kidneys, cook quickly both sides

Add mushrooms and plenty of freshly milled black pepper

Cook for further 2 mins

Add sherry and flame finish with clotted cream

Simmer gently until kidneys are cooked

Serve on a bed of rice

AROMATIC LAMB WITH APRICOTS
(from Rose & Crown, Harpley)

INGREDIENTS (SERVES 4)

1.5lb leg of lamb, boned and diced

2 onions, sliced

flour

oil

1 pt lamb stock

2 tsp ground ginger

1 tsp ground coriander

1 tsp ground cumin

1 tsp ground turmeric

rind & juice of 1 lemon

rind & juice of 1 orange

2 green peppers, sliced

4ozs dried (no soak) apricots

salt & ground black pepper

METHOD

Flour the lamb and fry in oil until browned - remove to casserole
Fry onions until browned and add all spices - fry briefly
Add stock and bring to boil, scraping up any sediment
Add to meat in casserole
Stir in fruit juices & rind, season with salt & pepper
Ensure liquid just covers meat; if not, top up
Place casserole in hot oven - 200°c for 30 mins
Reduce temp. to 170°c for one hour
Add apricots and sliced peppers, return to oven for 30 mins
Check meat is tender and seasoning correct

Serve on bed of rice or couscous, accompanied by mixed salad.

BEIGNETS OF COD BRANDADE WITH TEMPURA BATTER

(from The Three Horseshoes, Madingley)

INGREDIENTS

2lbs salted cod

6 garlic cloves

1 cup milk - warm

1 lemon

1 cup olive oil - warm

pepper & nutmeg

Batter:

6ozs flour

pinch baking powder

8-10 ice cubes

METHOD

Desalt cod in water, 4 - 5 hours
Poach cod in fish stock for 8 - 10 mins
Drain, skin and de-bone fish
Place fish in mixer, add garlic, milk & olive oil a little at a time
Add seasoning & lemon juice
Place on tray in fridge

Roll fish into balls
Roll in flour, dip in batter, fry for 2 - 3 mins

DO NOT SALT

WARM 'FRUITS DE MER'
(from Ben Handley of Titchwell Manor Hotel, Titchwell)

INGREDIENTS

9 fresh baby calamari

9 medallions of monkfish

12 prawns

4 king scallops

white wine

unsalted butter

8 - 12 keta (salmon eggs)

fresh marsh samphire

limes & fresh herbs (corriander, dill or chives)

4 saffron stamens

METHOD

Heat a small heavy pan until proved, add drop of olive oil

Sauté all the fish together until almost cooked

Add small amount of saffron & white wine and gently reduce

Thicken remaining licquor with unsalted butter

Add samphire & keta just before serving

Season to taste

Serve with limes & herbs

SALMON & TUNA FISHCAKES WITH CUCUMBER & PEANUT SAUCE

(from White Hart, Gt Yeldham)

RED CURRY PASTE:

4 stems lemon grass	4 red chillies
2 tsp ginger	4 shallots
6 cloves garlic	4 tsp coriander
2 tsp cumin	2 dsrt sp paprika

Place all ingredients in a blender and purée until smooth
Reserve, chilled in an airtight container

FISH CAKES:

10ozs tuna	6ozs salmon
2 tbsp coriander	2tbsp red curry paste
1 tsp lime juice	salt & pepper
1 green chilli, split, de-seeded and chopped coarsely	

Place all ingredients in food processor and pulse cut until roughly blended
Roll into small, round, flat balls and chill until needed
Lightly pan-fry these patties in virgin sesame oil until lightly golden
Best served immediately and a little pink

SAUCE:

2" cucumber	2 shallots
1 small carrot	1 small green chilli
1 tsp ginger	1 tbsp brown sugar
4 fl ozs mirren	1 tbsp soy sauce
1 tbsp ground nut oil	

Liquidise all ingredients until desired consistency is achieved, adding more sesame oil if required

RISOTTO OF SEA SCALLOPS

(from Le Talbooth, Dedham)

INGREDIENTS

8 large scallops (5 sliced, 3 diced)

11ozs risotto rice

1 shallot, peeled and finely chopped

olive oil

1 pint fish stock, boiling

1 tbsp freshly grated parmesan

1 carrot, peeled and cut into small dice
cook in alittle butter until al dente

2 courgettes cut into small dice
cook in a little butter until al dente

Salt & freshly ground white pepper

Lemon juice

2ozs double cream, lightly whipped

½oz finely chopped chives

few sprigs chervil

METHOD

Sweat the shallot in a tiny amount of olive oil in heavy-bottomed pan for a few mins
Add rice, stir for a few mins
Add ¾ of boiling stock and cook the rice, adding more stock if required
Keep the rice moving as much as possible to prevent sticking
When rice is ready almost all the liquid should have evaporated and grains should be al dente
Fry scallop slices very quickly in a little olive oil to sear and brown
Stir parmesan cheese, diced vegetables and diced scallop into risotto
Season with salt, pepper & lemon juice
Add cream & chives at very last moment and remove immediately from heat
To serve, place risotto in a bowl and garnish with scallop slices & chervil sprigs

PAUPIETTES OF SOLE FILLED WITH FRESH CRAB & SERVED WITH A PRAWN & GINGER SAUCE

(from Kevin Bingham of Duxford Lodge, Duxford)

INGREDIENTS (SERVES 4)

Sole:

4 double lemon sole fillets	4 tbsp fresh white crab meat
2 tbsp double cream	pinch cayenne pepper
lemon juice or lime juice to taste	salt & pepper
diced tomato	chopped chives

Prawn & Ginger Sauce:

450g prawn shells	1oz root ginger
1 onion, chopped	1 carrot, chopped
2 sticks celery, chopped	1 tsp tarragon
2 star annise	2 cloves garlic
200ml passata	150ml brandy & white wine
225ml double cream	seasoning
olive oil	

METHOD

Sole:
Mix together crab meat, cream, seasoning, cayenne pepper, juice
Place a tablespoon of crab mix between each double fillet of lemon sole and wrap with buttered clingfilm
Cook in a steamer for approx. 10 mins

Sauce:
In large heated pan put olive oil, chopped vegetables, ginger, garlic, herbs & spices
Cook for 5 mins
Add prawn shells and cook for another 10 mins
Add brandy & white wine, reduce by half
Add passata & cream, simmer for 45 mins
Sieve & season
You may need to adjust thickness of sauce
Presentation:
When lemon sole is cooked place on a pre-heated plate and pour the prawn sauce over.
Sprinkle with diced tomato & chive

PAPILLOTTE OF RED MULLET SCENTED WITH COURGETTE, LIME & TARRAGON

(from Kirk Ellingham, sous chef Knife & Cleaver, Houghton Conquest)

INGREDIENTS (SERVES 4)

four medium-size whole red mullets, or 8 fillets

12 purple shallots, peeled and diced

4 lime leaves, or 4 limes

4 sprigs tarragon

2 courgettes, ends cut off, diced

coarse sea salt

2 sheets greaseproof or tin foil

METHOD

Scale and fillet the fish carefully, as flesh is soft

With tweezers remove the little pin bones that run down the middle

Sprinkle fillets with lime juice and sea salt - leave

Cut greaseproof or foil into large heart shapes large enough to take two fish fillets on one side

Brush each heart shape lightly with butter

Sprinkle with shallots

Place a few leaves of tarragon on one side

Place two fillets on top of this

Sprinkle with diced courgettes & another spoonful of lime juice or a lime leaf

Fold paper in half until the edges meet, then fold tightly all the way round, leaving no gaps

Pre-heat oven to Gas Mark 7, 370°f

Place papillottes on a baking tray for 8 - 10 mins, or until edges are brown

Serve at the table, opening the parcel to release the scents and flavours - fish should be soft and courgettes still well coloured

CHOCOLATE TRUFFLE WITH SAUCE ANGLAISE
(from No 24 Restaurant, Wymondham)

INGREDIENTS

500g best quality chocolate, melted in double saucepan

0.5 litre whipping cream, lightly whipped

pinch of cinnamon

25g sultanas, blanched in 4 dessert spoons of Grand Marnier

sponge cake

METHOD

Gently fold the melted chocolate into the whipped cream
Add spice, sultanas & liqueur
Cut three discs from the sponge, suitable for the chosen mould
Simply place the sponge on the base of the mould and layer the chocolate truffle with the remaining sponge
Chill for a minimum of four hours
Remove from mould and dust with cocoa
Decorate with chocolate shavings
Serve with suitable sauce

SAUCE ANGLAISE

INGREDIENTS

4 egg yolks

50g caster sugar

½ litre boiling milk

METHOD

Cream together egg yolks and sugar
Pour milk onto this, return to stove until slightly thickened - DO NOT BOIL
Allow to cool; flavour with mint, hazelnuts, coffee, citrus zests or spirits

WHISKY TRUFFLES
(from Jason Shaw of Baumann's Brasserie, Coggeshall)

INGREDIENTS

1.8kg dark chocolate, melted
(couverture)

1 pint warmed whisky

300g double cream

200g glucose syrup

100g melted unsalted butter

METHOD

Boil together double cream, glucose syrup & butter
Remove from heat and gently whisk in melted chocolate
Add whisky, whisk gently until smooth & glossy texture
Pour into chosen tray & chill for 8 hours
Mould into desired shapes using a little cocoa powder
Then temper some more couverture and dip truffles

CARAMELISED LEMON TART
(from Shaun George, chef de partie, Crown Hotel, Southwold)

INGREDIENTS

1 baked blind pastry ring

2 lemons (zest & juice)

4 eggs

6ozs sugar

150ml double cream

1oz sugar for glazing

METHOD

Whisk eggs & sugar
Add juice & zest of lemons
Stir in the double cream and pour into the pastry shell
Bake at 150°c for 45 mins or until set
Remove from the oven and leave to cool
Chill in refrigerator

To serve, sprinkle the top with sugar and glaze with a blow torch or hot grill. Serve with creme fraiche & fresh berries

HONEY & WALNUT FLAN
(from The King's Head Inn, East Bergholt)

INGREDIENTS

8" sweet pastry base (cooked)

Filling:

3ozs butter

5ozs soft brown sugar

3 eggs

6ozs set honey

1 tsp vanilla essence

4ozs walnuts

METHOD

In a mixing bowl cream together butter & sugar until light and fairly smooth

In a separate bowl beat the eggs and add them gradually to the sugar & butter mixture

Mix in the honey & vanilla essence - don't worry if it curdles slightly, this is quite normal!

Spread the walnuts over the base of the pastry case and carefully cover with the honey mixture

Bake in a hot oven 175 - 200°c, Gas Mark 5, until set

Serve cold with cream

VANILLA & MANGO PARFAIT
(from Fen House, Littleport)

INGREDIENTS (FOR 10)

6 egg yolks

10 fl ozs double cream

4 ozs caster sugar

1 tsp vanilla essence

5 medium ripe mangoes, peeled and stoned

METHOD

Purée three of the mangoes
Add a little sugar if desired
Place in freezer
Whip the cream to stiff
Whisk together sugar, yolks & vanilla until white
Place over a pan of simmering water and continue to whisk until cool
Fold in the double cream and line a a pre-chilled mould with three quarters of the mixture, spreading it up the sides with a spoon
Freeze for about 15 mins to firm up
Stir the chilled mango purée and pour into the cavity made in the vanilla mix
Freeze again to firm up
Spread the remaining vanilla mixture over the purée to enclose it
Freeze
Dip the mould in hot water and turn out the parfait
Cut enough slices from the remaining mangoes to decorate, purée remains
Add sugar & water to produce a sauce
Portion the parfait, decorate and sauce around

BROWN BREAD ICE CREAM

(from Redcoats Farmhouse Hotel, Redcoats Green)

INGREDIENTS

1 pint double cream

6ozs caster sugar

3 egg yolks

1 dessertspoon liquid glucose (optional but prevents ice cream from being hard)

4ozs brown breadcrumbs

2ozs brown sugar

METHOD

Caramelise the breadcrumbs and sugar by putting them in a moderate oven until browned - leave to cool

Place in liquidiser or food processor and reduce to fine crumb texture

Cream together the eggs and caster sugar until pale creamy colour

Then add glucose (warmed to make it runny)

Add cream and whip up to thick consistency

Fold in breadrumbs and freeze

SANDRINGHAM PUDDING
(from Ffolkes Arms Hotel, Hillington)

INGREDIENTS (SERVES 12)

half cup Marsala

500g cooked chocolate sponge

1 litre milk

10 eggs

100g demerara sugar

1 tsp mixed spice

1 tbsp ground ginger

100g glace cherries

100g candied peel

100g diced apples

100g diced pear

100g toasted flaked almonds

finely grated zest of 1 orange & 1 lemon

METHOD

Place diced sponge in buttered dish
Sprinkle Marsala over sponge
Mix together all fruit, nuts, zest & spices and add to sponge
Make an egg custard with eggs, milk & sugar
Pour onto sponge mix and allow to soak for 10 mins
Bake at 160°c for 50 mins or until custard has set
Serve with vanilla ice cream

SEMOLINA BLANCMANGE WITH RASPBERRIES

(from Emma Parker-Williams, pastry chef, Swan Hotel, Southwold)

INGREDIENTS (SERVES 4)

16ozs flour

7 tbsp sugar

2.5ozs semolina

1 egg, separated

5ozs quark or low fat curd cheese

2 tbsp grated lemon rind

juice of one lemon

pinch of salt

8ozs raspberries

METHOD

Bring milk & 5 tablespoons of the sugar to the boil
Gradually stir in the semolina, bring to boil and simmer for 5 mins on very low heat

Mix the cheese with the egg yolk, 1 tablespoon of lemon juice and lemon rind
Combine with warm semolina mixture
Set aside to cool

Whisk egg white & salt until stiff - fold into cooling semolina

Rinse 4 dessert bowls in cold water and transfer the mixture to them
Leave to set in the refrigerator

Wash the raspberries in a bowl of water
Drain and mix them with the rest of the lemon juice & sugar
Chill in refrigerator

Unmould the individual blancmanges onto plates and surround with raspberries

▲▼▲

INNS & PUBS

▲▼▲

THE WHITE HORSE AT PLESHEY

Pleshey, nr Chelmsford. Tel: (01245) 237281

Location: south end of village, on main road near church.
Credit cards: Mastercard, Visa, Amex.
Bitters: Nethergate, Crouch Vale, Tolly Cobbold, guests.
Lagers: Carlsberg, Carlsberg Export, Dortmunder.

Examples of bar meals (lunch & evening, 7 days): *home-made soup; huffers; ja* *potatoes; daily specials eg fresh salmon in hollandaise, Thai curry, liver & ba casserole, pasta dishes. Bakewell tart; spotted dick; ginger pudding with lemon sau chocolate sponge; lemon brulée.*

Examples of restaurant meals (as above): *steaks & grills; fillet Wellington; rack of lamb; chicken Kiev; grilled whole lemon sole; French three-bean casserole; broccoli & cheese bake. Trad. Sun. roasts.*

The trendy "brand image" pub sadly continues to gain ground, but John and Helen Thorburn are sticking resolutely to the traditional values which have won them the respect of local people and most national guides over the past 10 years. That's not to say nothing ever changes: a new extension blends in superbly with the ancient original and leads out to the patio and large garden where there's a children's play area at the back; there's occasional live entertainment - could be musicians or magicians; every Saturday is specials night and ad hoc theme nights might include Thai, Indian and so on. The no-smoking restaurant is divided by timber lattices into four areas, very atmospheric, especially when the open fire is on the go - easy to believe in the phantom 'lady in blue'.

THE BLACK BULL FREEHOUSE
Dunmow Road, Fyfield, nr Ongar. Tel: (01277) 899225

Location: on B184 Ongar to Dunmow road.
Credit cards: Mastercard, Visa, Switch.
Bitters: Wadworth 6X, Courage Directors, Ruddles, John Smith.
Lagers: Fosters, Carlsberg, Kronenbourg.

Examples of bar/restaurant meals (lunch & evening, 7 days): *pork spare ribs with smoky barbecue sauce; haddock smokies; greenlip mussels in spicy blackbean sauce; steak & kidney pudding; wing of skate with lemon butter; seafood special; breast of duck with plum & brandy sauce; lasagne; chilli; steaks; daily specials eg home-made pies, liver & bacon, sea bream baked with fresh herbs & garlic, lobster salad. Fish night on Thursdays. Lunchtime only: jacket potatoes; variety of ploughmans; sandwiches; specials.*

The Black Bull is widely regarded as being one of the best pubs for food in these parts, so booking ahead is always advised at busy times. Proprietor (for 21 years!) Alan Smith has achieved this status by taking great pains to preserve high standards - deep frying is frowned on, and the menus are highly original and prepared with skill. The emphasis is on fresh meats, fish and vegetables, 'gently' influenced by chillies, garlic, coriander and other spices! Fish speciality night is Thursday, a chance to try oysters and lesser known varieties of fish. The building is over 600 years old - not immediately evident from the outside, but inside is rich with heavy timbers and open fires, and includes a separate dining area, ideal for parties of up to 30. The atmosphere is hospitable, the staff friendly and courteous.

THE WHITE HORSE
Norton Heath, nr Ongar. Tel: (01277) 821258

Location: off A414 between Ongar and Chelmsford.
Credit cards: Mastercard, Visa, Switch, Delta.
Bitters: Ruddles, John Smiths.
Lagers: Fosters, Kronenbourg.

Examples of bar meals (lunch & evening except Sat evenings): *rib eye steak in garlic butter; smoked seafood platter; breast of chicken with mushroom & red wine sauce; steak & Guinness pie; liver & onions; lentil cakes in tomato & pimento sauce; sandwiches; salads. Lemon & orange terrine; rice pudding.*

Examples of restaurant meals (lunch & evening, 7 days): *duck & chicken liver paté with pear & apple chutney; ravioli of fresh crab with tomato & chervil sauce. Lightly steamed fillet of red bream with roasted shallots on mild red chilli & balsamic sauce; roast saddle of venison with game sauce; daily specials eg poached fillet of salmon with crab mousse, fillet of beef Rossini. Chocolate & hazelnut mousse on café creme anglaise; fresh date tart; thin ginger shortbread sandwiched with raspberry cream on raspberry sauce. Trad. Sun. roasts.*

Although well known and respected as a restaurant, this 400-year-old coaching inn is in many ways the classic English pub, and indeed one is welcome to drop in for a drink without obligation to eat - but a glance at the menu will tempt you anyway. The split-level dining room is particularly fine, with exposed brickwork, timber lattices and French windows opening onto the large beer garden (with play equipment). Weddings etc are welcome; new owners Anna and Anthony Clarke and Chris and Karen Low have for many years run an outside catering service. No jukebox or piped music.

THE BELL INN & HILL HOUSE

High Road, Horndon-on-the-Hill. Tel: (01375) 642463 Fax: (01375) 361611

Location: village centre, main road.
Credit cards: Mastercard, Visa, Amex, Switch, Delta.
Accommodation: 14 dbls/twins; 2 with 4-posters, all en-suite, TV, phone, hair-dryer,
trouser press, tea & coff; £40 - £60 per room excl.
Bitters: Fullers London Pride, Highgate IPA, Bass, 8 local guests.
Lagers: Carling, Tennents, Tennents Extra.

Examples of bar meals (lunch & evening, 7 days): *braised lamb shank with garlic & rosemary; grilled pork chop with cabbage & meaux mustard; steak & kidney pie. Home-made desserts.*

Examples of restaurant meals (as above): *smoked salmon & vegetable strudel; chicken & pepper terrine wrapped in bacon; sautéed kidneys, poached egg & mustard sauce. Saddle of lamb baked in pastry with chicken tarragon mousse; fillets of red mullet on tomato tart pesto sauce; pigeon breasts with haggis & potato rosti; ratatouille harlotte with tomato salad. Trad. Sun. roasts.*

NB: menus change daily - separate lunch & dinner menus.

This lovely little village is in every sense elevated above the industrial flatlands of Essex, an oasis of peace and antiquity thought to be the final resting place of Ann Boleyn. Widely accepted as the best place to eat and drink (over 100 wines) for miles around and commended by most national gudes, the bustling Bell Inn is well endowed with period character, which permeates the busy and rather infectious atmosphere. There's a lined and carpeted marquee to the rear of the pretty courtyard, a small function room upstairs along with five individually decorated suites, and, just down the street, elegant Hill House, with another 10 well appointed bedrooms and a second, slightly larger function room.

THE HURDLE MAKERS ARMS

Post Office Road, Woodham Mortimer, nr Maldon. Tel: (01245) 225169

Location: off the A414 between Danbury & Maldon.
Credit cards: (purchases over £15) Mastercard, Visa, Switch, Delta.
Bitters: Greene King IPA & Abbott, occasional guest.
Lagers: Stella Artois, Carlsberg, Kronenbourg.

Examples of bar meals (lunchtimes only, 7 days): *steak & Guinness pie; chicken balti; lasagne; salmon koulibac; crevettes in garlic butter; mussels in garlic butter; ploughman's; sandwiches; daily specials eg duck & orange paté, wild smoked venison, Moorland smoked trout, pork & cider pie, beef bourgignon. Sticky toffee apple & fudge cake; home-made profiteroles; fruit pies; pavlovas. Trad. Sun. roasts.*

It's all too easy to miss this delightful little 17th-century pub (recently acquired by Victoria and Jason Murrell), tucked away as it is a few hundred yards off the A414. It would be a shame to do so for it has much to offer, not least the two acres of attractive garden with children's play area. Such a spread readily accommodates barbecues on Sundays and Bank Hols. There's also a pitch-and-putt driving range to the rear. Inside you'll find two lovely oak-beamed bars with flagstone floors, settles dotted round tables and an open fire - the Grey Lady and Black Monk have seemingly eschewed paradise to linger on here! The food is fresh, almost entirely home-made and served in generous portions. Darts, dominoes and shut-the-box. Toilet for the disabled.

THE BELL
Woodham Walter, nr Maldon. Tel: (01245) 223437

Location: village centre, 2 miles off A414.
Credit cards: not accepted.
Bitters: Adnams, Friary Mieux, Young's Special, Kilkenny, guest.
Lagers: Carlsberg, Lowenbrau.

Examples of bar meals (lunch & evening daily except Sundays & Mon evenings): *steaks & grills; curries; chicken Kiev; lamb cutlets; salmon & broccoli pie; duck in orange sauce; mushroom & spinach tagliatelle; ploughman's; sandwiches; daily specials eg steak & kidney pie (noted), liver & bacon, prawn jambalaya. Chocolate cheesequake; crepes suzettes; apple pie; banana split.*

They don't come more traditional than this! The Tudor era lives on in this remarkably well preserved pub, built a quarter of a century before the Spanish Armada; heavy oak timbers and panelling, leaded windows, back-to-back bench seating in the gallery dining room - all very evocative, as are the old photos dotted about. One picture promptly fell off the wall when landlord Alan Oldfield had the temerity to say that the place isn't haunted - he has since had second thoughts. He and wife Margaret took over in 1992 to make The Bell a freehouse for the first time in 200 years. Serving unpretentious, fresh home-made food and well kept ales they have won recognition from CAMRA and the Good Pub Guide. They welcome children and have a family room most of the week - it doubles up for functions and overspill at peak times. No jukebox or piped music. Garden to rear.

THE BULL

2 Maldon Road, Gt Totham, nr Maldon. Tel. & Fax: (01621) 893385

Location: southern part of village, on B1022 towards Maldon.
Credit cards: Mastercard, Visa, Diners, Amex, Switch, Delta, JCB.
Bitters: Burtons, Flowers, Tetley, Kilkenny, 2 guests.
Lagers: Carlsberg, Carlsberg Export, Labatts, Castlemaine.

Examples of bar/restaurant meals (lunch & evening, 7 days): *home-made chicken liver paté; steak & kidney pudding; kleftico; chicken medley; confit of duck leg; rack of lamb; pork coriander; baked ham with mustard sauce; lasagne; chilli; 1lb whole sea bass chargrilled; steaks & grills; speciality curries; vegetable & cheese Wellington; fresh fish specials Weds & Thurs. Bread & butter pudding; lemon meringue; pavlova; chocolate gateau; banoffee pie. Children's menu. Trad. Sun. roasts £7.95 (4 courses).*

NB: over 55's Privilege Menu on Mons & Tues; £2.75, £3.50, £4.75 (1, 2 & 3 courses).

A previous landlady (Mabel Crumpton) refused service to anyone who tripped over the entrance step - bad luck if you just happened to be clumsy. These days customers may trip over themselves, but only for the good, value-for-money food which, despite the extensive menu (chalked up on blackboards all around the lounge bar), is home-made and cooked to order - curries are the speciality of landlord Ray Ibbotson. Since 1993 he and wife Carole have run this early 18th-century inn overlooking a cricket green and The Blackwater beyond. To the rear the bright and airy restaurant (available for functions) overlooks the garden. Children welcome. Public bar has pool, darts and Sky TV.

THE Du CANE ARMS
The Village, Gt Braxted, nr Witham. Tel: (01621) 891697

Location: village centre.
Credit cards: Mastercard, Visa, Delta, Switch.
Bitters: Greene King IPA, Adnams, Websters, John Smith, 2 guests.
Lagers: Carlsberg, Fosters, Holsten.

Examples of bar meals (lunch & evening, 7 days): *fresh fish of the day (chef's own beer batter); chef's home-made steak, kidney & mushroom pie; beef midani; chicken princess; lasagne; steaks; trout; caprisciosa fettucini (seafood); salads; sandwiches. Home-made fruit crumbles; treacle pud; spotted dick; chocolate pud; pavlova; roulades; banoffee pie.*

Examples of restaurant meals (as above): *chef's own paté; home-made soups; pork Madagascar; plaice fleurie; rossini; noisettes of lamb with stilton & mint sauce; fresh grilled cod or haddock with orange & tarragon glaze; chicken supreme with ginger & cream sauce; vegetable midani (midanis a speciality). Trad. Sun. roasts.*

NB: Bar meals may be enjoyed in restaurant for a £1 cover charge.

Fresh herbs and vegetables in season from the garden, fresh-baked rolls from the oven, interesting and predominantly home-made food (the uncommon midani dishes are particularly popular): The Du Cane Arms is drawing custom from a wide radius to this out-of-the-way village. The Hyde family - Eric and Brenda, Alan and Angela - came here in spring 1991 with many years of experience. Their high standards refreshingly extend to a ban on foul language. There has been an inn on the site since 16th century, when the Du Canes were the local gentry, but this one dates from the 1930s, and is light and airy, with pot plants in the L-shaped bar, fresh flowers in the restaurant (which also serves for functions up to 30). Small garden. Pottery opposite, Braxted Hall and golf course nearby.

THE SQUARE & COMPASSES

The Green, Fuller Street, nr Fairstead. Tel: (01245) 361477

Location: turn off A131 at Gt Leighs, follow Boreham Road towards Terling.
Credit cards: not accepted.
Bitters: Ridleys IPA & ESX, winter ale, guests (on stillage).
Lagers: Carlsberg, Carlsberg Premium.

Examples of bar meals (lunch & evening, 7 days): *home-made gravadlax; grilled mackerel in spicy tomato sauce; fish pie; poached skate with brown butter & capers; steak & kidney pie; cottage pie with leek & cheese crust; venison sausages braised in red wine & onions; steaks; mushroom & onion quiche; salads; ploughman's; jacket potatoes; sandwiches (noted); daily specials eg bowl of jellied eels with cottage roll, lemon pepper chicken breast, monkfish wrapped in bacon, local game in season. Lime cheesecake; chocolate truffle mousse; fruit pavlovas & meringues; sponge puddings. Trad. Sun. roasts in winter.*

If you thought the true country pub an endangered species, you will be cheered to discover this fine, friendly example of the genre alive and well in the back lanes of a pretty part of Essex, popular with walkers on the Essex Way. The mainstay is good, straightforward English cooking, using local produce as much as possible; bread is fresh and 'real', game a speciality. Mysteriously once known as the Stoke Hole, the pub's cottage origins have not been lost; an array of woodworking instruments and old photos look just right in this setting. Patron Saints' days are celebrated with live music, and a glass of mulled wine makes a winter's night very acceptable. The landlord (since April '95) has a good name for outside catering - marquee possible. Large garden, plans for petanque and other improvements.

THE GREEN DRAGON

Upper London Road, Young's End, nr Braintree.Tel: (01245) 361030 Fax: (01245) 362575

Location: A131 2 miles south of Braintree - nr Essex showground.
Credit cards: Visa, Mastercard, Diners, Amex.
Bitters: Greene King Abbot & IPA. Bottled selection.
Lagers: Harp, Kronenbourg.

Examples of bar meals (lunch & evening, 7 days): *steak, kidney & mushroom pie; leek, mushroom & potato cakes; curry; chicken dumplings; daily specials eg apricot-stuffed pork fillet in filo pastry with green peppercorn sauce, spicy meatloaf, smoked sprats in mustard sauce, plaice fillet stuffed with asparagus & smoked salmon. Spotted dick; treacle sponge; fruit sorbets.*

Examples of restaurant meals (as above) *sea bass in filo pastry with sorrel sauce; drunken bullock; roast duckling with Cointreau sauce; chicken & bacon parcels; kleftiko; fillet of lamb with cassis & blackcurrant sauce; steaks; brown rice & hazelnut loaf. Trad. Sun. roasts.*

Bob and Mandy Greybrook have been at the Green Dragon for over 12 years, during which time it has become one of the most popular pubs in the area (the large car park is a necessity) and the recipient of numerous catering awards. Fresh seafood - langoustines and salmon from Scotland, oysters and wetfish from nearby Mersea - has increasingly become a speciality. The 48-seater restaurant was converted from a barn, serving a la carte and fixed-price menus (table d'hote is just £13.50 incl.), plus a Sunday roast menu throughout the day - bookings always advised. Or just drop by for a meal in the cosy bar or snug. The garden has a play area with aviary. Private parties and weddings catered for.

WHITE HART PUB & RESTAURANT
Gt Saling, nr Braintree. Tel. & Fax: (01371) 850341

Location: on main road, village centre.
Credit cards: Mastercard, Visa.
Bitters: Ridleys.
Lagers: Holsten, Fosters, Heineken.

Examples of bar meals (lunch & evening, 7 days): *Desperate Dan steak & kidney pie; liver & bacon; steaks, chilli; merguez sausages with fries & onions; balti with naan; huffers. Cointreau creme brulée; bread & butter pudding; treacle pud; chocolate & rum mousse.*

Examples of bakehouse restaurant meals (lunch & evening Wed - Sun, except Sat lunch & Sun evening): *Colchester mussels in herb broth; grilled black pudding with asparagus in basil dressing; fillet of salt beef carpachio "White Hart". Skate fillet with bacon, cornichons & capers; roast pheasant with sauerkraut & brandy gravy; stir-fried mixed vegetables & mushrooms with egg noodles. Trad. Sun roasts plus alternatives.*

"The home of the huffer" has graduated well beyond this very popular and tasty snack. They are still served, crammed full of various fillings, but now this epitome of the English country pub (used in the filming of 'Lovejoy') also presents dishes of the kind one might expect in Michelin Star restaurants - indeed, the chef has worked in a few in different countries. His creativity is further demonstrated on theme nights, such as Cockney or Wok-frying (sometimes with live music), and he can also call on fresh home-grown organic vegetables and herbs - it does make a difference. "Corporate Days" are a clever innovation for small businesses: outings are organised around clay pigeon shoots, go-karting, Newmarket races etc, with food laid on. Piped music. Play equipment in garden. Saling Hall and Gardens and Blake End Crafts very near.

THE PRINCE OF WALES

Brick End, Broxted. Tel: (01279) 850256 Fax: (01279) 850738

Location: between Takeley and Elsenham, nr Stansted Airport.
Credit Cards: Mastercard, Visa, Amex.
Bitters: Friary Mieux, Kilkenny, guest.
Lagers: Lowenbrau, Castlemaine.

Examples of bar/restaurant meals (lunch & evening, 7 days): *terrine of mixed smoked fish; filo parcels of Austrian smoked cheese with gooseberry puree; timbale of citrus fruits with peach & blueberry coulis; pan-fried strips of chicken & smoked salmon finished with cream & tarragon; Cumberland sausage on bubble & squeak with onion gravy; whole plaice with dill & lime juice; broccoli & walnut roulade with red pepper sauce; chunky sandwiches (lunch only); vegan choices; daily specials eg barbecued spare ribs. Bread & butter pudding laced with rum; crepe basket filled with white Belgian chocolate topped with maple syrup. Children's menu. Trad. Sun. roasts.*

In the same family hands for almost 20 years, this early Victorian freehouse is quietly tucked away in pleasant countryside, yet only minutes from the airport. The huge car park is a necessity - good, imaginative, home-made food (feted in national newspapers), on a menu continually revised, at very modest prices, will always be a winning formula. Holders of the new Midweek Privilege Card enjoy even better value. The stylish conservatory, with its tent-effect ceiling, serves as a most agreeable restaurant and family room (suitable for small weddings etc), but one may eat in the characterful split-level timbered bar (the upper tier is a second restaurant). The rear patio has a play area. Piped music. Audley End and Tilty Abbey nearby.

THE CROWN
Elsenham, nr Bishop's Stortford.Tel: (01279) 812827

Location: village centre.
Credit cards: Mastercard, Visa, Diners, Amex, JCB.
Bitters: Crouch Vale Millennium Gold, Tetleys, guest (changed regularly).
Lagers: Carlsberg Export, Castlemaine, Carlsberg.

Examples of bar meals (lunch & evening daily except Sundays): *deep-fried bread baskets with various fillings; savoury stuffed pancakes; seafood mixed grill; sautéd chicken livers in crepe basket; steak & kidney pie; lamb turino; duck Marco Polo; fisherman's pie; vegetable lasagne; pork T-bone in Calvados; local fresh trout in shellfish sauce; steaks; daily specials eg barbecue ribs, fresh plaice filled with crab & prawns, casseroles. Lunch only: homemade Crown burgers; Braughing sausages (noted); chicken tikka. At least 15 home-made ice creams. Trad. Sun. roasts with fish alternatives. Menu revised regularly.*

The sheer extent and originality of the menu makes it all the more amazing that everything, even the ice cream, is home-made and fresh. This has not escaped the notice of most of the main national guides and especially that of local people, so booking is advised at peak times. All is of course cooked to order, but there are a number of quick items listed for those in a hurry at lunchtime. Around 350 years old, formerly three cottages and then a coaching inn (royalty is said to have stayed here), its antiquity can be seen in the split-level bar, with its old timbers and open fire, next to which is the intriguing 'Dingly Dell', a floral fantasy. Activity comes in the form of monthly quiz nights, darts and dominoes. Well behaved children welcome. Dining room available for wedding receptions (and funerals!). The patience and good humour of licensees Ian and Barbara Good is witnessed by over 22 years of pulling pints here.

THE CRICKETERS ARMS

Rickling Green, Quendon, nr Saffron Walden. Tel: (01799) 543210 Fax: (01799) 543512

Location: on village green.
Credit cards: Mastercard, Visa, Diners, Amex.
Accommodation: 10 dbls/twins (incl. 1 bridal suite); all en-suite, TV, phone, hair dryer, trouser press, tea & coff; from £50 sngl, £60 dbl incl; airport parking.
Bitters: Flowers IPA, guest strong beer, also usually a mild.
Lagers: Hoegarden, Stella Artois, Carlsberg, Leffe.

Examples of bar/restaurant meals (lunch & evening, 7 days): *Rickling paté; extrava-ganza of smoked fish; spicy vegetables; continental sausage platter; fish soup. Chicken in apricot & cream sauce; black pudding in mustard sauce; home-baked gammon in port & orange sauce; cottage pie; liver & bacon; steak & kidney pie; fresh fish dishes of the day; steaks & grills; vegetarian ravioli; mussels dishes; balti curries; jacket potatoes; sandwiches, ploughman's; daily specials eg poached wild salmon in cucumber sauce, chicken Kiev. Oranges in Cointreau caramel; chocolate cup; steamed syrup sponge; pineapple fritters with hot apricot sauce; gateaux. Children's menu. Trad. Sun. roasts plus alternatives.*

Essex County Cricket team plays on this marvellous village green one Friday every June. Players always repair to this ever popular inn, run by Tim and Jo Proctor for the past 11 years. Prodigious amounts of food are prepared in Jo's kitchen; the menu comes in the form of a booklet, and there are numerous daily specials besides, but it's fresh and cooked to order. Although outwardly Victorian, the interior of the building looks much older. Bedrooms are equipped to modern standards - useful to know if flying from Stansted. Well suited for functions (marquee available). Children welcome. Live duos planned for Friday evenings.

THE CRICKETERS

Clavering, nr Saffron Walden. Tel: (01799) 550442 Fax: (01799) 550882

Location: on B1038, village outskirts.
Credit cards: Mastercard, Visa, Amex, Switch, Delta.
Accommodation: 2 dbls, 4 twins; 2 with 4-posters, all en-suite, TV, phone, hair dryer,
trouser press, tea & coff; £60 sngl, £80 dbl.
Bitters: Flowers Original & IPA, Boddingtons Gold, guest.
Lagers: Heineken, Labatt, Stella Artois.

Examples of bar/restaurant meals (lunch & evening, 7 days): *salad bar; parcels of pasta filled with crabmeat & spring onions, served with crab bisque; gazpacho Andalux; duck liver & pink peppercorn terrine with Oxford sauce. Fillet of sea bream grilled with light ginger butter sauce; loin of pork stuffed with stilton & apricots in Armagnac sauce; mixed vegetable curry. Trad. Sun. roasts.*

Trevor and Sally Oliver found this a bikers' haunt; 20 years on, it's universally recognised as amongst the very best in the region, succeeding both as a fine country pub and quality restaurant. Stability and staff loyalty have played an important role. The building itself hasn't changed too much either: a combination of low ceiling and sloping floor will catch the unwary, and leaves one in no doubt that this is a very old place - 16th-century in fact. The attractive restaurant (available for functions) is more recent, but blends in perfectly. 'Pub of the Year' and other certificates testify to prowess in the kitchen - all is fresh and prepared on the premises. Just across a rather pretty garden is the 'Pavilion', in which are the large, individually designed bedrooms - handy for Stansted, Cambridge etc. Family room.

THE AXE AND COMPASSES.

Arkesden, nr Saffron Walden. Tel: (01799) 550272

Location: village centre.
Credit cards: Mastercard, Visa.
Bitters: Greene King IPA & Abbot.
Lagers: Kronenbourg, Harp.

Examples of bar/restaurant meals (lunch & evening, 7 days): *chicken, leek & bacon crumble (speciality); steak & kidney pie; moussaka; lamb kebabs with tomato & basil sauce; pork loin on mushroom sauce glazed with stilton; sweet & sour chicken; halibut on leek sauce; foccacia; pasta dishes; steaks; mushroom pancake with cheese & cream sauce; sandwiches. Raspberry & hazelnut meringue; chocolate & Grand Marnier mousse; fruit pies; spotted dick. Trad. Sun. roasts £12 (4 courses).*

NB Children eat at half price.

"One of the finest pubs in Essex" was the verdict of the Daily Telegraph, a view endorsed by Michelin, AA and other major good pub guides. Arkesden is a dream of a village: grand old thatched houses straddle a little stream in the dappled shade of willow trees - it puts many a more famous place to shame. For complete perfection a lovely old country pub is required, and 'The Axe and Compasses' fulfills the role admirably - a picturebook 17th-century house, presided over by owner Themis Christou and family. They foster a notably relaxed and unhurried atmosphere, aided by crackling fires in winter, so linger a while and savour the home cooking from four chefs! (headed by Phil Hayburn). Children welcome in restaurant and patio areas. Definitely not one to be missed.

THE WAGGON & HORSES

High Street, Gt Yeldham, nr Halstead. Tel & Fax: (01787) 237936

Location: on A604, 200 yds from famous Yeldham Oak.
Credit cards: Mastercard, Visa, Delta, Switch, Amex, Diners.
Accommodation: 1 sngl, 5 dbls/twins. TV, tea & coff. c/h. £15pp
incl Cont. brkfst. Rooms are 16th-century.
Bitters: Greene King, 1 regional & 1 national guest.
Lagers: Harp, Kronenbourg.

Examples of bar snacks (lunch & evening, 7 days): *deep-fried potato skins; scampi; plaice (with hand-cut chips); doorstep sandwiches; ploughman's.*

Examples of restaurant meals (as above): *filo basket filled with creamy garlic mushrooms; hot bacon, walnut & avocado salad. English lamb chops with apricot & brandy sauce; steak & kidney pudding; half roast duck with honey & thyme; halibut steak in white wine, cream & herb sauce. Lemon meringue pie; treacle tart; apple pie. Trad. Sun. roasts £9.95 (3 courses).*

The eye-catching painted waggon to the front was the Rolls Royce of its day; built in 1840, it is one of the oldest in the country. Another outmoded transport is the nearby Colne Valley Steam Railway. Being 'Lovejoy Country' the area has an association with antiques, with many fine buildings, of which this former three 16th-century cottages is one. Two ghosts are said to walk the timbered, split level bar, one of them a lady who apparently objects to war memorabilia but not the many Punch cartoons with amusing modern 'punch lines'. Young chef Ellie Cox is highly regarded in the area, and her cooking utilises as much fresh and local produce as possible. Young and affable landlord Mike Shiffner has built a thriving business since Nov. 1994, and plans further improvements. Games Room has pool, darts and shove ha'penny; garden has boules. Children welcome. Accommodation is remarkably good value.

THE BELL INN
St James Street, Castle Hedingham. Tel: (01787) 460350

Location: village centre.
Credit cards: not accepted.
Bitters: Greene King, Shepherd & Neame Spitfire, Master Brew, guests.
Lagers: Heineken, Kronenbourg.

Examples of bar meals (lunch & evening daily, but no food Mon evenings except Bank Hols, or Sun evenings in winter except holidays): *home-made paté; mussels in garlic butter with wine & cream; liver & bacon casserole; steak & Guinness pie; shepherds pie; chicken kebabs; fisherman's pie; ham & broccoli bake; sirloin steak; canneloni; pizza; Thai chicken curry; salmon steak with dill & lemon juice; NZ greenlip mussels; huffer; lamb burger; ploughman's; mushrooms in garlic butter. Banoffee pie; treacle tart; bread pudding. New on Fri & Sat evenings & Sun lunch: barbecue fish specials (many exotics).*

Things don't seem to change much in this pretty, historic little village. After the castle The Bell is the second oldest building, its 15th-century origins (although the staircase to the cellar is pre-1400) remarkably in tact: solid oak beams, authentic brickwork, wooden floorboards. This rare continuity extends to landlady Sandra Ferguson, now in her 30th year here. Good home-made food, beer straight from the barrel and a friendly welcome have secured a regular place for many years in major national pub guides and local esteem. The venerable timbers vibrate to live jazz on the last Sunday of each month (12:30 to 3:15pm, entry free) and acoustic guitar on Friday evenings (plus Sunday evenings at Bank Hols). Children welcome - no-smoking bar, restaurant and family room. Lovely walled orchard garden.

THE GREEN MAN
Gosfield, nr Halstead. Tel: (01787) 472746

Location: on A1017 Braintree to Hedingham road.
Credit Cards: Mastercard, Visa, Amex, Switch, Delta.
Bitters: Greene King.
Lagers: Kronenbourg, Castlemaine.

Examples of bar meals (lunchtime 7 days, every evening except Sunday): *Every day lunch & evening: game soup with sherry; breaded mushrooms with garlic butter; Dover sole; oxtail ragout; steaks; boiled beef & carrots; roast duck with orange sauce; plaice fillets with prawn sauce; steak & kidney pudding; selection of home-made fresh vegetarian dishes (eg spinach pancakes, vegetable lasagne). Lunchtime additional: Cold buffet; choice of locally & home-made desserts.*

'Essex Dining Pub of the Year' is a recent accolade from a leading national good pub guide for the best traditional food in the county. Nothing is frozen; all is cooked to order - special requests catered for if possible. You may not be able to resist the succulent array of cooked meats, shellfish, salmon and more on the buffet table, and speciality evenings - eg Italian, Greek, Curry, Fish - are also very popular, so booking is advised. It's refreshing to see staff so well turned-out, courteous and hard-working. Tellingly, most have worked for proprietor John Arnold for many years, including his 'right-hand lady', Janet Harrington, now in her 27th year here. It is these 'old-fashioned' virtues which endow this 16th-century pub with uncommon warmth and civility. Children are tolerated if well behaved; if not there's a rather nice garden by the large car park. Small room for private functions.

THE KING'S HEAD
The Street, Gosfield, nr Halstead. Tel: (01787) 474016

Location: main road, village centre.
Credit cards: Mastercard, Visa, Delta, Switch.
Bitters: Wadworth 6X, Boddingtons, Flowers IPA, Marstons Pedigree, guest.
Lagers: Stella Artois, Heineken.

Examples of bar meals (lunch & evening, 7 days): *rib-eye steak; kleftico; pan-fried salmon; spare ribs; liver & bacon; baguettes; salads; ploughman's. Banoffee pie; strawberry shortcake; tiramisu; summer fruit pudding; pear Belle Helene.*

Examples of restaurant meals (as above): *home-made chicken liver paté & Cumberland sauce; smoked salmon parcels filled with smoked mackerel mousse; spinach & cream cheese mousse with pimento sauce. Steak Hongraise; chicken en croute with whole grain mustard sauce; escalope of pork picarta; plaice Veronique; vegetarian dish of the day. Trad. Sun. roats plus alternatives.*

New owners (since July '97) have made rapid strides in restoring the fortunes of this striking 15th-century traditional village inn (once a police station!), managed by Cheryl Gadd. Weekly revised menus are chalked on a blackboard; the home-produced food (nothing bought in) and relaxed atmosphere are bringing the customers back in droves. The 70-seater conservatory restaurant (children welcome) is a fine setting for a memorable meal, or indeed a wedding reception (private functions welcome). Darts and pool in public bar. Patio to front and rear. Hedingham Castle and Gosfield Lakes (with water skiing) are very close.

THE SWAN INN
Chappel, nr Colchester. Tel. & Fax: (01787) 222353

Location: just off A604, near viaduct.
Credit cards: Mastercard, Visa, Switch, Delta.
Bitters: Greene King, guest.
Lagers: Carlsberg, Carlsberg Export, Stella Artois.

Examples of bar/restaurant meals (lunch & evening, 7 days): *smoked salmon with prawns; mushrooms stuffed with liver paté; Swan seafood special; deep-fried rock eel; steaks & grills; ploughman's; sandwiches; salads; rolls; daily specials eg salmon in honey & dill, grilled sea bass, scallops & bacon, Danish herrings. Fruit pavlovas & tortes; banoffee pie; chocolate fudge cake; profiteroles; cheesecake.*

In a dramatic setting, almost under the colossal arches of England's longest railway viaduct, this ever popular 14th-century inn is special in a number of ways: the River Colne runs through the large garden (and sometimes over it), and there has been a ford (and probably an inn) here since Roman times; it has one of the best preserved medieval kitchens in the country (no longer in use!); and the owner (for 17 years) also has a wholesale fish business, hence the outstanding quality of fresh seafood, simply prepared, accompanied by a good wine list. One may enjoy it in the very agreeable no-smoking restaurant, in the timbered bar with its huge fireplace (lit in winter), or you could even dine al fresco in winter in the remarkable heated courtyard. Well behaved children welcome; adventure playground. Functions up to 28. East Anglian Railways Museum very near.

THE KING'S HEAD

Burnt Oak, East Bergholt, nr Colchester. Tel: (01206) 298190

Location: east side of village - follow signs to Flatford.
Credit cards: Mastercard, Visa, Switch, Delta.
Bitters: Greene King IPA, Flowers Original, Kilkenny, guest.
Lagers: Carlsberg, Stella Artois.

Examples of bar/dining room meals (lunch & evening 7 days from May to Sept; no food Sun evenings and Mon evenings in winter): *fresh salmon & dill paté; honey & mustard chicken; Cajun grilled pork; steak & kidney pie; chicken, bacon & tomato pasta bake; pork & apricot pie; lamb Madras; steaks; lasagne; chilli; moussaka; salads; jacket potatoes; ploughman's; baguettes; Friday fish specials; Saturday night extras eg lamb brochette, poached salmon, pork in Dijon mustard & cider sauce. Bakewell tart; dark & white chocolate cheescake; treacle tart with almonds; honey & walnut flan. Trad. Sun. roasts.*

Constable's paintings evoke a nostalgia for a lost, arcadian past. But all is not entirely lost: this lovely village, very near the famous Flatford Mill, has resisted 20th-century encroachments, and its fine 18th-century pub, in which the great painter may well have supped, has also not succumbed, remaining independent and free of the modern blight of trendy themes and formula food. It is home to Nicki and Phil Woodend (proprietors since 1994 and both experienced in catering); the lounge bar could almost be their front room, with displays of china, cottagey furnishings and of course Constable prints. One may eat there or in the pleasant dining room with its vaulted wooden ceiling. Food is home-cooked and menus chalked up daily, but this is not a restaurant and drinkers are welcome. Good value wines. Pool table in Public Bar. Nice garden.

THE COMPASSES INN
Ipswich Road, Holbrook. Tel: (01473) 328332 Fax: (01473) 327403

Location: on main road in village centre.
Credit cards: Mastercard, Visa, Diners, Amex.
Bitters: Benskins, Tetley, guest.
Lagers: Stella Artois, Carlsberg.

Examples of bar/restaurant meals (lunch & evening, 7 days): *crab bake; breaded mushrooms; paté; melon cocktail; kleftico; steaks; seafood & traditional lasagne; chicken curry; chicken Alexander; home-made pies; fresh fish daily; smoked fish-cakes; daily roast; jacket potatoes; salads; sandwiches; vegetarian selection; many daily specials. Treacle pud; cherry pancakes; chocolate & rum gateau. `Booking advised, particularly weekends.*

Travellers once hired ponies here for the journey to Ipswich, which was a safer mode of transport than by boat on the River Orwell, to judge from the engraved ships' timbers dredged up and put into use. Hanging from the beams are more than one thousand key fobs - you are welcome to check! The remarkable Victorian restaurant (no-smoking), with its very uncommon domed ceiling, may be hired for private parties and weddings - balloons and banners provided. However, what really makes the Compasses so popular are the generous portions of good, home-made food at very reasonable prices. Children are allowed and have a play area outside; grown-ups can relax in the garden or on the patio. In the same hands for over 17 years, the pub features regularly in national guides.

BUTT AND OYSTER

Pin Mill, Chelmondiston, nr Ipswich. Tel: (01473) 780764

Location: off B1456 Shotley Road.
Credit Cards: Mastercard, Visa, switch.
Bitters: Tolly Cobbold - on handpump or from barrel, from the reborn
brewery across the river. Occasional guests.
Lagers: Stella Artois, Carlsberg.

Extended Hours: **Winter:** Mon-Fri 11am-3pm, 7pm-11pm; Sun 12 -3pm, 7pm-10:30pm. **Summer:** Mon-Fri 11am-11pm; SATS & SUNS 11am-11pm ALL YEAR.

Examples of bar meals (lunch & evening, 7 days): *lamb puffs; smoked haddock & prawn pot; smoked chicken, celery & walnut pie; spinach & ricotta cheese lasagne; fisherman's pie; smoked chicken with onion & chive dip; savoury sausage pie; pork & apple pie; steak & kidney pie; tiger tail prawns; crispy curry pancakes; honey roast half duck; farm manager's lunch. Pecan pie; lemon brulée; toffee meringue. Buffets at Saturday & Sunday lunch. Limited menus (rolls etc) outside main hours.*

Views of the River Orwell such as this are a major asset. However, not content to rest on nature's laurels, Dick and Brenda Mainwaring work at keeping the Butt and Oyster authentic. They succeed, as national guides and newspapers testify, and CAMRA named this the 'Regional Pub of the Year 1993.' The locals also treasure it, and the elders will confirm that it is unchanged over 60 years. Even the pub games, some almost forgotten elswhere, live on here; juke boxes and the like do not. The view from the bar and dining room overlooks the boats and river, and at very high tides the river nearly overlooks them. There's an old smoke room with bare floorboards and smoke-stained ceiling. The home-made food varies daily and is of generous proportions. There's a children's room, or sit at tables by the river's edge.

THE ANGEL INN

Stoke by Nayland, nr Colchester. Tel: (01206) 263245 Fax: (01206) 263373

Location: village centre.
Credit cards: Mastercard, Amex, Diners, Visa.
Accommodation: 6 doubles, all en-suite, TV, phone, hair dryer, tea & coffee;
£60 per room incl. (£46 as sngl).
Bitters: Adnams, Greene King.
Lagers: Carlsberg, Kronenbourg.

Examples from lunch & supper menu (served daily in bar & Well Room, where table may be booked): *fresh dressed crab; home-made fishcakes; tomato & feta cheese salad; wild boar sausages; steak & kidney pudding; honey-glazed roast rack of lamb; sauté of liver & bacon; griddled fresh wing of skate; steamed fillets of salmon & halibut; roast ballantine of duckling. Apple, apricot & sultana jalousse; raspberry & vanilla bavarois; syrup pudding. Trad. Sun. roasts. All is freshly prepared on the premises.*

'Which?' Suffolk Hotel of the Year 1997 joins a long list of accolades (won over the past 13 years under current ownership), which include Egon Ronay's Pub Accommodation of the Year Award 1995 (for the whole country), and Suffolk Dining Pub of the Year in another major good food guide. The Angel is simply one of the most celebrated inns of the region, if not the entire country. Although the Georgian facade is attractive enough, it is but a prelude to the very splendid 17th-century interior. Looking for the most outstanding feature, one would settle on the gallery which leads from the tastefully appointed bedrooms to a view over the restaurant. A charming little lounge divides the bars from the two dining rooms, one of which has an ancient well. The village is a very pretty one, in the heart of Constable Country and just 15 minutes' drive from Colchester.

THE GEORGE & DRAGON
Hall Street, Long Melford. Tel: (01787) 371285 Fax: (01787) 312428

Location: centre of village, on main road.
Credit cards: Mastercard, Visa, Switch.
Accommodation: 2 sngls, 4 dbls/twins, 1 family; all en-suite, TV, direct phone; special breaks by arrangement.
Bitters: Greene King, guest.
Lagers: Kronenbourg, Castlemaine.

Examples of bar/restaurant meals (lunch & evening, 7 days): *melon & prawn fan served on fruit sauce; game terrine. Swordfish steak on fresh lime sauce; halibut with white grapes in Muscadet sauce; roundels of lamb with hot mint sauce; pork & apple pie; kidney bordelaise; beef in Abbot ale; Suffolk sausages with onion gravy; smoked chicken with pasta; steaks; vegetarian dishes; sandwiches; daily specials. Desserts.*

NB: OPEN ALL DAY, EVERY DAY.

"Not a pub, not a restaurant, but a true village inn" - the words of Peter, Marilyn and Ian Thorogood, who've revived the art of innkeeping at their 16th-century coaching inn over the past 12 years. That means "no karaoke, discos, keg beer or men in oversized suits drinking from bottles!" Instead, you have delicious and filling meals created in the kitchen from fine local produce, traditional local beers and superb French wines (clarets especially good). Entertainment, too, is traditional, with live music every Wednesday. Look out for special commemorative dinners - St George's Day, for example. Well behaved children are welcome, and there is a garden. An ideal base to stay; right in the heart of the region, Long Melford is England's longest village, a Mecca for antique collectors, and boasts two Tudor Halls and Suffolk's finest church. Recommended by most major pub guides.

THE ANGEL HOTEL
Market Place, Lavenham. Tel: (01787) 247388 Fax: (01787) 248344

Location: town centre.
Credit cards: Mastercard, Visa, Amex, Switch.
Accommodation: 7 dbls/twins, 1 family; all en suite, TV, phone, hair dryer, tea & coff; from £65 per room (from £39.50 as sngl) incl. special midweek breaks.
Bitters: Adnams, Nethergate, Mauldons, Greene King.
Lagers: Holsten, Carlsberg.

Examples of bar/restaurant meals (lunch & evening, 7 days): *warm salad of pigeon breast; smoked haddock bake; sausage cassoulet & granary bread; steak & ale pie; braised rabbit with white wine, tomatoes & rosemary; pheasant braised with cider & apples; grilled salmon fillet with pickled samphire; lamb in paprika & cream; sirloin steak; leek, tomato & lentil gratin. Raspberry creme brulée; Drambuie & oatmeal syllabub; chocolate roulade. Trad. Sun. roasts.*

Good Pub Guide's "Pub of the Year" and "Suffolk Dining Pub" (both 1997); Which? "Suffolk Hotel of the Year" 1995; an AA Rosette for cooking; regular inclusion in all the major national guides; more important, loyal customers who keep coming back - testimony to the high standards set over eight years by Roy and Anne Whitworth and John and Val Barry. Yet prices remain very reasonable indeed for such a location (on a corner of the famous market square, often used as a backdrop for historical movies), and the atmosphere always relaxed. Neither are children frowned upon; indeed, toys, high chairs, a no-smoking area and even friendly cats are all laid on! Older ones may appreciate the many board games provided, or even, one hopes, the classical pianist on Friday evenings. Look for the magnificent exposed Tudor fireplace and rare Tudor shuttered shop window. Tables and benches to the front and in attractive rear garden with patio and barbecue.

THE PLOUGH INN
Brockley Green, nr Hundon, nr Clare. Tel: (01440) 786789 Fax: (01440) 78671

Location: 1 1/2 miles from Hundon towards Kedington (not to be confused with Brockley Green on the B1066); if in doubt, phone.
Credit cards: Mastercard, Visa.
Accommodation: 7 twins/dbls, 1 family; all en-suite, teletext TV, phone, hair dryer, trouser press, tea & coff; weekend breaks £175 for 2 people, 2 nights dinner, B & B. ETB 4-Crown; member of Logis; Caravan Club certified location.
Bitters: local traditional ales, weekly guest.
Lagers: rotating premier & standard.

Examples of bar meals (lunch & evening from 6pm, 7 days): *home-made soups; beef & Guinness pie; fresh fish; steaks; ploughmans.*

Examples of restaurant meals (as above): *lemon sole with prawns; duckling breast with orange; steaks; salmon poached in wine & cream; vegetarian dishes; seafood night every Tuesday. Trad. Sun. roasts (booking advised).*

Now in their 16th year here (it's been in the family over 30 years), David and Marion Rowlinson, ably assisted by Jim and Margaret Forbes, provide modern amenities (the restaurant is plush and air conditioned, for example) without sacrifice of old fashioned friendliness and charm. Soft red bricks and oak beams from an old barn engender a country pub atmosphere; this and good home cooked food (seafood a speciality) has won a place in local affections and a number of major guides. Not an easy one to find, but patience reaps its rewards. The views over the rolling countryside are alone worth the effort, and there is also a south-facing landscaped terrace garden. Well placed for Cambridge, Bury St Edmunds and Lavenham. Children welcome.

THE CROWN

The Green, Hartest, nr Bury St Edmunds. Tel: (01284) 830250

Location: by the village green.
Credit cards: Mastercard, Visa.
Bitters: Greene King Abbot, IPA & seasonal beers.
Lagers: Kronenbourg, Carling.

Examples of bar meals (lunch & evening, 7 days): *home-made brandy & chicken liver paté; smoked salmon & prawn paté; fresh Cromer crab; whole fresh brill with prawns in parsley butter; fresh fish & chips (take-away); vegetables grilled in breadcrumbs with barbecue sauce; salads; omelettes; sandwiches; daily specials eg mixed grill, breast of chicken in au poivre sauce, lamb grilled with rosemary. Home-made sherry trifle; plum & apple crunch; banana & toffee cheesecake; chocolate bombe. Trad. Sun. roasts.*

Picturebook cottages around a village green in a tranquil little fold; medieval church amongst tall trees; wonderful old country pub serving good, home-made food and beer: here is the English 'dream scene'. This 15th-century inn fits the bill to perfection: oak panelled, beamed, ornate fireplace, inglenook lit in winter, walls hung with original paintings (by David Ashworth, uncle of landlady Karen Beer). Karen and husband Paul have, over six years, made this one of Suffolk's most popular pubs, highly commended by most national guides. The three dining rooms are often full, but service is brisk, the atmosphere friendly. A new room, which opens onto the lawn, is ideal for wedding parties (coaches also welcome). Special menus (eg Shellfish, American) are laid on every Monday evening except Bank Hols. Children's play area in large garden.

THE PLOUGH

The Green, Rede, nr Bury St. Edmunds. Tel. (01284) 789208

Location: cul de sac, not far from church.
Credit cards: Mastercard, Visa.
Bitters: Greene King.
Lagers: Harp, Kronenbourg.

Examples of bar meals (lunchtime every day, & evenings except Sunday): *fresh fish (speciality); steaks; curries; salads; daily specials eg jugged hare in port & wine sauce, romany lamb with spaghetti & parmesan cheese, beef in horseradish sauce, chicken ham & stilton crumble.*

Examples of restaurant meals (evenings only, not Sundays. Traditional Sunday lunch): *pigeon breasts in Madeira & spinach; venison; trout; roast duck; veal in Dijon mustard & brandy; poached salmon; local game (speciality).*

Here in a quiet cul de sac by the village pub is the quintessential thatched country pub for which England is renowned, in the heart of some of Suffolk's finest countryside. Unlike some others, no disappointment awaits inside: the inglenook fireplace is an especially handsome one, the beams look good for another 500 years, and the fine collection of teapots strikes the right note without lapsing into tweeness. More importantly, the food is good and portions very substantial - The Plough has been a regular in good pub guides for years. Amiable hosts Brian and Joyce Desborough and staff foster an unstuffy, unhurried atmosphere, but in summer you may prefer the large sunny garden with a tropical aviary, a dovecote and ponies - children love it! They are welcome inside in the eating areas.

THE CHERRY TREE
Bury Road, Stradishall. Tel: (01440) 820215

Location: On A143 Bury to Haverhill road.
Credit cards: Mastercard, Visa.
Bitters: Greene King Abbott & IPA, Wexford.
Lagers: Kronenbourg, Carling.

Examples of bar/dining room meals (lunch & evening, 7 days): *steaks; pasta; king prawns in garlic butter with coconut rice; Suffolk pork & apple pie; chicken breast cooked with cream & madeira; filled jacket potatoes (lunch only); baguettes (lunch only); ploughman's (lunch only); daily specials eg minted lamb in red wine, traditional steak pudding, peppered salmon fillet with lime butter, poached smoked haddock with cream & chive sauce, crab tart. Home-made chocolate & brandy truffle cake; lemon & marshmallow cheesecake; butterscotch pudding with rum sauce. Trad. Sun. roasts plus alternatives.*

One of the joys of exploring our lovely countryside is the occasional chancing upon a quite delightful little country pub. Here in the heart of rural Suffolk is one such. Set in over four very pleasant acres, including a large fish pond (complete with resident ducks), this cosy 16th-century timbered farmhouse became a pub only in 1943, taking the place of another which unfortunately was in the way of pilots taking off from RAF Stradishall! Since then there have been only four landlords, the latest being local people Jane and Roger Marjoram, with over 20 years' experience in the trade. Their menus are a commendable blend of staple English favourites with a little foreign zest. Separate dining room. Handy for Newmarket, Cambridge, Bury St Edmunds, Clare, Long Melford and Lavenham.

THE BEEHIVE
Horringer, nr Bury St Edmunds. Tel: (01284) 735260

Location: on A143 Haverhill Road.
Credit cards: Mastercard, Visa, Switch, Delta.
Bitters: Greene King.
Lagers: Carling, Kronenbourg.

Examples of bar meals (lunch & evening, 7 days): *Caesar salad with Scandinavian crayfish tails; smooth chicken liver & chunky bramley apple paté; wild mushroom risotto with creme fraiche; Thai-style chicken curry with fragrant coconut rice; pancake filled with flaked smoked haddock, cheese & cream served with salad bowl; baked fillet of salmon with peanut crust, ginger & chilli butter, with salad bowl & new potatoes; Beehive steak sandwich; hot spicy ratatouille with cheesy garlic bread; ploughman's; daily specials eg fresh lobster salad, escalope of pork in creamy stilton sauce. Chocolate bread & butter pudding; treacle tart; banana cheesecake with toffee nut sauce.*

The name is apt: situated almost at the gate of Ickworth Hall, this 300-year-old flint cottage fairly buzzes; after 12 years in the hands of Gary and Diane Kingshott it is one of the best known and loved eating places in the area, featured in all the leading national guides. The reputation has been built on quality food, freshly and imagina-tively prepared yet quickly served, but you will be equally welcome if you just fancy a pint. The small, timbered, rambling rooms, with antiques and old prints, are cosily inviting, or one may sit in the garden. You could even take the short drive to Gary and Diana's recent acquisition, The Queen's Head, Kirtling (qv) for desserts! Children welcome.

THE TROWEL & HAMMER INN
Mill Road, Cotton, nr Stowmarket. Tel: (01449) 781234 Fax: (01449) 781765

Location: east side of village; from Stowmarket turn right off B1113 at signpost.
Credit cards: Mastercard, Visa, Eurocard, Delta, Switch, JCB.
Bitters: Adnams, Greene King, Nethergate, guest.
Lagers: Kronenbourg, Carlsberg.

Examples of bar meals (lunch & evening, 7 days): *filos of brie with creamy chive sauce; grilled sardines with herb butter; avocado salad with chicken & prawns; crab & herb pancakes; liver & bacon with onion gravy; fresh deep-fried cod with chips; steaks; kleftico; creamy leek, potato & stilton pie; steak, kidney & ale pie; ploughman's.*

Examples of restaurant meals (restaurant closed Sun. evenings & Mons): *terrine of salmon with watercress & dill; escalope of salmon with spinach & hollandaise sauce; confit of duck perigordin; fillet steak en croute. Pancakes with blackcurrants & cassis; chocolate & Cointreau mousse in brandy snap. Trad. Sun. roasts.*

This 15th-century freehouse, one of the best known and most picturesque in the region, was acquired in May '95 by Simon Piers-Hall (formerly of the wine trade) and Julie Huff (formerly of the celebrated Royal Oak, Yattendon). It is gratifying enough that it should continue as a family concern, but they have also introduced exciting menus, always freshly prepared despite their broad scope and daily revision, and accompanied by an outstanding wine list. In winter lovely open fires broadcast good cheer; in summer you may prefer to splash in the swimming pool in the large garden. There's also indoor pool - the kind played on a flat table. The cosy oak-beamed restaurant is well suited to private parties, and there's occasional live music. Well-behaved children welcome.

THE MILL INN

Bury Road, Market Weston, nr Diss. Tel: (01359) 221018

Location: on B1111 between Stanton and Garboldisham.
Credit cards: Mastercard, Visa.
Bitters: Old Chimneys (local), Adnams, Greene King.
Lagers: Carlsberg, Kronenbourg.

Examples from lunch menu (Tues-Sun): *Sri Lankan beef curry; raised chicken & ham pie; smoked haddock & broccoli mornay; steak & stout pie; pasta provencale; salads from around the world; sandwiches; daily specials eg Dover sole Florentine, ham & leek roly poly with onion gravy; trad. Sun. roast plus 8 alternatives. Home-made fresh fruit pavlova; rum & raisin pie; chocolate brownie with chocolate custard; cherry brandy trifle; home-made ice creams.*

Examples from evening menu (Tues-Sat): *home-made venison paté; stir-fry prawns with mustard & coriander; duck breast with plum sauce; home-made vegetable ravioli & tomato sauce; steaks & grills: Turkish lamb; supreme of chicken stuffed with crab meat & coated with prawn & white wine sauce; daily specials.*

NB: closed ALL DAY Mondays except Bank Hols.

So many country pubs have either closed or fallen into the wrong hands of late that it is doubly refreshing to report one which gives cause to hope. Since taking over in September 1995, Mother and daughter Anne and Lesley Leacy (both with catering diplomas and experienced in the art) continue to make their mark with good, fresh, home-made food at very reasonable prices, served with a genuine friendliness in bar or dining room of their 18th-century former miller's home. The good-size menus are international enough, but monthly theme nights (usually on Thursdays) introduce diners to French, American, Curry etc specialities. For extra fun join in one of the car treasure hunts, or take a tour around a 'Mill Trail' of local windmills. Children's room and garden. Outside catering service.

THE BLACK HORSE INN & STABLES RESTAURANT

The Street, Thorndon, nr Eye. Tel & Fax: (01379) 678523

Location: 2 miles off A140 Norwich to Ipswich road at Stoke Ash.
Credit cards: Mastercard, Visa, Delta.
Bitters: Greene King Abbot & IPA, Woodfordes Wherry, Wexford, guest.
Lagers: Kronenbourg, Carlsberg.

Examples of bar/restaurant meals (lunch & evening, 7 days): *hot baps eg beef & onion with Worcester sauce; steaks & grills; curry; chilli; lasagne; steak & kidney pie; mushroom stroganoff with cream & brandy; jacket potatoes; ploughman's; salads; sandwiches; many specials eg sirloin steak in stilton sauce, breast of chicken with white wine & hazelnut sauce, king scallops in white wine & shallot sauce, tuna steak in white wine & herbs, halibut steak with white wine & prawn sauce. Home-made cheesecakes; sticky toffee pudding; chocolate pudding; fruit pies. Children's menu. Trad. Sun. roasts.*

Built in the 16th century to service travellers (there was once a ferry across a nearby lake), this freehouse enjoys a good name for home-cooked specials chalked daily on a blackboard. Vegetarians are well looked after, fresh and crispy vegetables being a forte. Value for money is outstanding; half a pound of mince goes into each lasagne, for example, and the large oval plates are well filled. The restaurant has been cleverly converted from stables, and the stalls are singularly conducive to intimacy and good conversation in a friendly atmosphere, assisted by a log fire in winter. Children like to peer down the 42' well (covered by plate glass!) in the heavily timbered bar, and there's a lawned garden with seating. Occasional Morris Dancing and Pony and Trap meets. Beers notably fresh and well kept.

THE RAMSHOLT ARMS
Dock Road, Ramsholt, nr Woodbridge. Tel: (01394) 411229

Location: off B1083 Woodbridge-Bawdsey road.
Credit cards: Mastercard, Visa.
Accommodation: 4 twins/dbls, £35pp B & B; tea & coffee; TV & hair-dryer on request.
Bitters: Adnams, Flowers, Brakspears.
Lagers: Heineken, Stella Artois.

Examples of bar/restaurant meals (lunch & evening, 7 days, except Dec, Jan & Feb, when no food Sun evenings): *warm salad of breast of woodcock & partridge with plum sauce; big bowl of fresh mussels with chips & mayonnaise; beef tomato with feta cheese, black olives & fresh basil. Fresh halibut pan-fried in olive oil; pot-roast partridge with red cabbage, bread sauce & game chips; platter of fresh local lobster, oysters, whole prawns & wild Irish salmon; fillet of pork poached in cream with lime & juniper. Belgian chocolate mousse; sticky toffee pudding; fresh meringue; bread & butter pudding. Trad. Sun. roasts.*

Winner of the Egon Ronay "1997 Newcomer of the Year" award, this former shooting lodge and smugglers' inn benefits from unrivalled views up and down the River Deben, being set by the beach at Ramsholt Dock. But paramount is the quality of the food: as much local produce as possible is used, and the daily-changing menu always includes fresh fish and game in season. Children are welcome in the comfortable bar, which has a log fire, or the quieter dining room overlooking the river. Newly refurbished bed-and-breakfast accommodation is very sought after - book well ahead. A new waterside marquee is available for functions - a stunning location for a wedding reception.

THE KING'S HEAD
Front Street, Orford. Tel: (01394) 450271

Location: village centre, by church.
Credit cards: Mastercard, Visa.
Accommodation: 2 dbls, 1 twin; all en-suite, TV, tea & coff; £45 incl. per room.
Bitters: Adnams, Adnams Extra, Broadside, seasonal.
Lagers: Carlsberg, Stella Artois.

Examples of bar/dining room meals (lunch & evening, 7 days): *Orford cod & chips; French onion tart; Orford smoked fish platter; chicken & pistachio nut paté; avocado & artichoke salad; Cromer crab salad; beef, venison & mushroom pie; fisherman's pie (noted); skate wing in burnt butter & capers; confit of duck with potato & mushroom sauté; braised sausages in red wine with bubble & squeak; pasta & bean crumble; broccoli & cauliflower cheese bake; salads; sandwiches. Treacle & muesli tart; chocolate truffle cake; lemon fromage frais cheesecake; warm orange pudding with Grand Marnier sauce. Trad. Sun. roasts in winter only.*

New owners Derrick and Dee Tipple have quickly reversed a period of decline which preceded their arrival in November '96; good news for this unique, exquisite village. The revival has been based on a happy atmosphere and fresh food of largely local provenance, cooked by Dee herself. Since the 13th century the pub has stood on a corner of the famous little village square, backing on to the church grounds - a smugglers' tunnel is said to link the two. All the rooms are bursting with character; the good-sized bedrooms (2 have sofas) are immaculate and have large bathrooms. Live music performed Saturday nights. Children welcome in dining room (available for functions) or garden.

THE GOLDEN KEY
Priory Road, Snape, nr Aldeburgh. Tel: (01728) 688510

Location: from the north turn left at bottom of hill.
Credit cards: Mastercard, Visa, Switch, Delta.
Accommodation: 1 dbl, 1 twin; both large and with sofas; both en- suite
(huge bathrooms), TV, hair-dryer, tea & coff; £55 per
room incl, £45 for stays of 5 nights.
Bitters: Adnams, seasonal.
Lagers: Stella Artois, Carlsberg.

Examples of bar meals (lunch & evening, 7 days): *cream of courgette soup; prawns in filo pastry; home-made liver paté; steaks; chicken breast in garlic butter; steak, mushroom & Guinness pie; sausage, egg & onion pie (noted); fresh fish grilled, with sauces; spinach quiche; vegetable lasagne; salads; ploughman's; sandwiches. Chocolate brandy cake; toffee crunch cheesecake; treacle & walnut tart; hot lemon cake. Trad. Sun. roasts.*

"Civilised" is a word which comes readily to mind at this delightfully tranquil early 16th-century inn, tucked away in a country lane just yards from the famous Maltings. There are no indoor games, no jukebox, no piped music; in fact very few concessions to the 20th century at all (save for the very well appointed bedrooms upstairs). But there is plenty of character and much to engage the interest, including an unusual semi-circular settle in front of one of the superb open fires, an ornate carved lintel (dated 1480), and a pagan-looking carved overmantle in the dining room (where children are welcome, and which serves for functions). But it is the cooking which prompts customers to travel miles. Some dishes (notably the pies) are so popular that Max and Suzie Hissick-Jones dare not remove them from the blackboard, even after 20 years! For the last 14 of those The Golden Key has been praised by Egon Ronay, and is also a regular in CAMRA and Good Pub Guide.

THE CROWN AT WESTLETON

Westleton, Saxmundham. Tel: (01728) 648777 Fax: (01728) 648239
INTERNET E-MAIL: reception@the crown.nemesis.co.uk

Location: village centre.
Credit cards: Access, Amex, Diners, Visa.
Accommodation: 17 doubles, 2 singles, private facilities & no-smoking in all. AA 2* 75%.
Tourist Board 3 Crowns highly commended. Class 2 access for disabled.
Bitters: Adnams, Woodfordes Wherry, Black Sheep, 3 guests.
Lagers: Carlsberg, Red Stripe. Plus James White & Scrumpy Jack ciders.

Examples of bar meals (lunch & evening except Sat evenings): *very fresh fish of the day (min. 5 dishes, cooked in various ways - speciality); steak & kidney pie; pork casserole with cheese & herb dumplings; sirloin steak; vegetable & cashew nut bake; salads; sandwiches; daily specials. Raspberry & apple sponge pudding; sweet trolley. Children's menu. Trad. Sun. roasts.*

Examples from a la carte menus (evenings only): *Greek egg & lemon soup; grilled king prawn sausage on salad leaves with balsamic dressing; roast sea bass with crispy fried leeks on jus of tarragon; prime fillet of beef with stilton, on crouton with rich port wine sauce; fruity vegetable & almond curry. Booking advised.*

Perhaps the only true coaching inn left; leave your nag to graze in the rear meadow (with two stables) while you holiday. Rosemary and Richard Price offer up-to-date amenities for humans too: six Honeymoon rooms, some with four-posters or half-tester beds, all equipped with superb bathrooms complete with Jacuzzi. Barbecues are held weekend lunchtimes (weather permitting) in the pleasant terraced garden, and a large conservatory is for the use of non-smokers. Inside there's an open log fire which spits and crackles on a cold day - just right for a bowl of soup and a hunk of granary bread, baked on the premises. World famous Minsmere Nature Reserve is just a few minutes' walk from this picturesque village.

THE WHITE HART
Blythburgh. Tel & Fax: (01502) 478217

Location: on east side of A12.
Credit cards: Mastercard, Visa, Switch (with minimum spend).
Bitters: Adnams, Kilkenny.
Lagers: Carlsberg, Stella Artois, Castlemaine.

Examples of bar meals (lunch & evening, 7 days): *fresh fish specials eg deep-fried skate wing; chicken breast in white wine & cream; steak & kidney pie; fresh prawns & mussels; salads; rolls. Bakewell tart; treacle tart; rhubarb crumble; fresh strawberries.*

Examples of restaurant meals (Thurs - Sat evenings, plus trad. Sun. roasts): *mozzarella salad with avocado; fresh salmon baked in foil; breast of Aylesbury duck with port; mushroom & tomato layer; various steaks; poached skate in butter & caper sauce.*

One of the very oldest inns of the region (1170) has acquired a new landlord: Nigel Harrison set out on this, his first venture in the trade, only in September 1996. He vows to observe the best traditions of Suffolk hospitality, and to present with care only fresh, home-made food - no freezer-to-microwave shortcuts. He also plans to develop the acres to the rear, for the views out over the Blyth estuary, just yards away, are quite stunning at high tide. The interior is also easy on the eye, with a fine original ceiling, large open log fire, back-to back settles and pictures for sale. The dining room, with fresh flowers and a magnificent inglenook, also serves for functions. The restless ghost of a judge is said to stalk this former courthouse; perhaps he misses the ducking stool to which he sent many a nagging wife! Children welcome. Petanque.

THE KING'S HEAD
High Street, Southwold. Tel: (01502) 724517

Location: main street, on right as approaching.
Credit cards: Mastercard, Visa.
Accommodation: 3 dbls/twins (non-smoking); all en-suite, TV, tea & coff;
from £50 per room; single rate by negotiation.
Bitters: Adnams.
Lagers: Stella Artois, Carlsberg.

Examples of bar meals (lunch & evening, 7 days): *local fresh fish simply grilled; steak & kidney pie; Orford honeyroast ham; oak-smoked gammon; chicken & asparagus pie; curries; chilli; lasagne; charcoal grilled steaks, fish & chicken; pasta & vegetarian dishes always; jacket potatoes; ploughman's. Bakewell tart; fruit crumbles; sticky toffee pudding. Trad. Sun. roasts.*

Southwold is famed for its easy-going pace of life, and dining at this 18th-century town-centre pub is intended to be a casual, "come as you are" affair. Flexibility is the watchword: any reasonable request will be met, and as everything is prepared to order be ready to wait a little while in peak periods. Use the time to quaff some of the excellent Adnams ales or wines, which travel only a few yards from the brewery in the town (the pub won the Adnams Cellar Award two years running), or study the pictures in the split-level timbered bar (formerly a grocery store). Sunday evenings are for Jazz and Blues buffs, when they are performed live. New bedrooms are very good value (as is the home-cooked food); take a brisk stroll to the beach before breakfast. Phil Goodacre is your genial host. Parking on street or nearby public car park. STOP PRESS: the pub will have a new Pizza Restaurant.

THE CROWN HOTEL & RESTAURANT
Crown Road, Mundford. Tel: (01842) 878233

Location:	village centre, just off A1065.
Credit cards:	Mastercard, Visa, Diners, Amex.
Accommodation:	from £32.50 sngl, £49.50 dbl; Coach House with beautifully appointed rooms & reception room.
Bitters:	Woodfordes Wherry & Nelson's Revenge, Websters, local-brewed Iceni beers, Sam Smiths, Directors.
Lagers:	Fosters, Carlsberg, Holsten Export, Kronenbourg.

Examples of bar meals (lunch & evening, 7 days): *chicken breast with bacon & stilton cream; leek & gruyere strudel on fresh tomato sauce; home-made lamb kebabs; fresh fish (speciality) with classic & unexpected sauces; many daily specials eg Hungarian chicken, poached fillets of sea bream on bed of asparagus with light cream sauce, parcels of broccoli bound with pasta in smoked cheese & onion cream sauce. Deep apple bakewell; tiramisu; chocolate & almond torte.*

Examples of restaurant meals (as above): *scallop & mange tout salad; field mushrooms & hot garlic cottage prawns; noisettes of lamb with fresh mint & balsamic vinegar; sea bass fillet with smoked marlin. Trad. Sun. roasts. Booking always advised.*

NB: Open all day; food served 12 to 3pm, 7 to 10pm (last orders).

The Crown's recognition in the principal national guides is firmly based on the cooking - anything from home-made soups to a classic medley of Ickburgh duck, served in typical Norfolk portions, with prices starting at under £2. Many regulars have also been gained through 'Norfolk Pub Walks' (this being good walking country). In its time (from 1652) The Crown has also been a hunting lodge and doctor's surgery, and, perhaps uniquely in Norfolk, is built on the side of a small hill, so that one may walk in to the ground floor bar and exit from the first floor restaurant into the garden - glorious in summer. A lovely inn to stop off for good food, lively company and comfortable accommodation.

THE CROWN INN FREEHOUSE & RESTAURANT
Church Street, Gt Ellingham. Tel: (01953) 452367

Location: 80 yards past church.
Credit cards: Mastercard, Visa, Delta, Switch, Euro.
Bitters: Woodfordes, Adnams, Theakstons, John Smith, Websters, guest.
Lagers: Fosters, Miller, Kronenbourg.

Examples of bar/restaurant meals (lunch & evening, 7 days): *unusual home-made pies; steaks; balti chicken; tagliatelle verdi with smoked bacon & cream; chilli; fresh fish direct from Lowestoft or Billingate; herb crepes filled with camembert cheese, seasonal veg. & tomato, basil & garlic sauce; salads (with h/m dressings & chutneys); omelettes; home-made baguettes; jacket potatoes; many daily specials eg grilled goats' cheese with Italian salami, duo of mallard & partridge casseroled with root vegetables & red wine. Home-made pancakes filled with fruit; choux pastry swan filled with chocolate mousse; jam roly poly; fruit pie. Children's menu. Trad. Sun. roasts.*

All credit to Justin Wilkins and chef Mark: despite a choice of 60-70 dishes, nothing on the main menu is bought in frozen and even the baguettes and chutneys are home-made. His four years here have helped make The Crown one of the most popular and respected eating houses in the area - a far cry from the days before the Wilkins family, who have lived in the village for generations, took over in 1989. Their remarkable success has resulted in a new extension (opened autumn 1997), where diners will be able to enjoy a pre-dinner drink while scanning the huge menu. The beer garden is due for landscaping and the patio for a canopy. But the original building, 250 years old, timbered, with huge fireplace and resident spectral monk, will remain undisturbed. Regular wine-tasting events. Butterfly farm nearby.

THE BIRD IN HAND
Church Road, Wreningham. Tel: (01508) 489438

Location: village centre.
Credit cards: Mastercard, Visa, Amex.
Bitters: Adnams, Bass, Caffreys, Fullers London Pride, Woodfordes Wherry,
John Smiths, weekly guest.
Lagers: Stella Artois, Heineken, Fosters, Miller, Gorlsch

Examples of bar meals: (12 to 2pm, from 6.30pm, 7pm Suns, until 10pm): *steamed Scottish mussels with garlic, parsley, lemon & white wine; stir-fried ratatouille, tomato, & spinach lasagne; chargrilled chicken breast marinated in honey, garlic grain mustard & lime juice; blackend cajan shark steak served with a spicy orange & piri piri dressing.*

Examples from a la carte: (12 to 2pm, 7 to 10pm, 7days): *roast French duck breast stuffed with oranges & chestnuts, served with cranberry & ginger chutney; sauteed monkfish with a garlic red wine, bacon & mushroom sauce; fillets of sole stuffed with spinach, served with a rich lobster sauce & on steamed samphire; roast rack of lamb served on a bed of Mediterranean vegetables & with a honey & rosemary sauce.*

This has emerged in recent years as one of the region's most talked about pubs, winning glowing praise from national publications and competition judges. Yet Carol Turner arrived nine years ago armed only with a training from the British Institute of Innkeeping and Norwich City College, and high expectations; now she has a staff of 30, including three chefs. The business continue to grow whilst maintaining the high standards of service and extensive menus on which its reputation has been built. The beautiful interior far surpasses the promise of the exterior, and is quite exceptional. The bar was once a stable, and that special farmhouse ambience is unmistakable; the restaurant is even called the Farmhouse, and is furnished most handsomely. Well behaved children welcome, and there's a large landscaped beer garden. Weddings and private parties a speciality. Conference facilites. Excellent washrooms.

THE WILDEBEEST ARMS
Norwich Road, Stoke Holy Cross. Tel: (01508) 492497

Location: village centre, 2 mins off A140, 5 mins city centre.
Credit cards: Mastercard, Visa, Switch, Delta, Diners, Amex.
Bitters: Adnams, Courage Directors, John Smiths.
Lagers: Fosters, Holsten, Kronenbourg.

Examples of bar meals (lunch & evening, 7 days): *terrine of ham knuckle with green peppercorns & frizze walnut salad; griddled smoked salmon with avocado tartar & lemon oil; twice-baked spinach & cheddar soufflé with rocket & parmesan; roast cod with lentils & bacon, pomme Anna & red wine sauce; rump of lamb with ratatouille, pesto & basil juice; baked asparagus & broad bean tart with sauce ravigote. Chocolate brownie; classic lemon tart with creme fraiche; mixed berry nougatine with strawberry & Grand Marnier coulis. Daily specials. Trad. Sun. roasts. 'Menu du Jour' (3 courses for £12). Plainer food for children on request.*

It caused quite a stir when it opened in autumn 1994, but it was no flash in the pan; The Wildebeest is firmly established, ever popular and now recognised by major national guides. A glance over the few examples listed above indicates why: original and adventurous, it could hardly be described as typical pub food, and you can watch its preparation in the open kitchen. The selective wine list is well priced and of good quality. A distinctive African theme is established (although not overstated) in the long, single bar by authentic musical instruments and wood carvings. Because of its popularity booking is always advisable. The Wildebeest is one of the group which includes the new Aquarium restaurant (qv) in Norwich. Children welcome. Garden.

THE KING'S HEAD
Bawburgh, nr Norwich. Tel: (01603) 744977 Fax: (01603) 744990

Location: village centre.
Credit cards: Mastercard, Visa, Switch, Amex.
Bitters: Fuggles, Adnams, Marstons Pedigree, Boddington,
Flowers IPA, Original, Courage Directors, 3 guests.
Lagers: Stella Artois, Kronenbourg, Mc Ewans.

Examples of bar/restaurant meals (lunch & evening, 7 days): *Provencal fish soup; cod frikadeller; wild mushroom risotto; grilled fillet of lemon sole with carrot, lime & coriander; shredded ostrich fillet stir-fried with sesame seeds, soy sauce & honey with rice; beef pie in real ale with herb gravy; baltis; pasta; kebabs; salads; baguettes; sandwiches. Chocolate delice; shortbread chantilly; bread & butter pudding. Children's menu. Trad. Sun. roasts.*

Much more than just a pub - The King's Head is a rarity, not just for the four squash courts and Crown Green bowls, but also for the highly creative and unusual food. Whether staunchly traditional, such as sausages and mash, or exotica like kangaroo or ostrich, all is fresh and prepared with pride by head chef Paul Shepherd. The choice of beers and wines is also exceptional. The inn has stood by the river running through this quaint little village since 1602, and is full of character. No games machines assault the senses, neither do cigarettes in the no-smoking room. Lee Vasey plays live alternate Monday evenings, and there are numerous special themes and promotions. Landlady Pamela Wimmer is joined in the business by son Anton. Function room for up to 80. Children welcome. Sheltered courtyard.

THE UGLY BUG INN
Colton, nr Norwich. Tel: (01603) 880794

Location: in village
Credit cards: Mastercard, Visa, Switch, Delta, Eurocard.
Accommodation: 1 single (£27), 1 twin (en suite), 1 family with
bathroom (both £45). Tea & Coff.
Bitters: Ugly Bug, Adnams, Old Speckled Hen, John Smith, 3 guests.
Lagers: Carlsberg, Kronenbourg.

Examples of bar/restaurant meals (lunch & evening, 7 days): *home-made paté; supreme of chicken stuffed with mozzarella in wild mushroom sauce; salmon in puff pastry with lemon & parsley sauce; pie of the day; ravioli stuffed with ricotta & spinach; home-made black pudding pan-fried in garlic butter; lasagne; curries; steaks. Apple & marmalade crumble; lemon & mascarpone cheesecake; treacle pud; summer pud; quality Swiss ice creams. Trad. Sun. roasts £8.95.*

The odd name is not at all apt, for this striking conversion stands in over three acres of the most beautifully landscaped gardens (with barbecue), complete with carp stream and floodlit bridge. Inside, you will find it warm and congenial, replete with timbers, exposed brickwork and cottagey furniture. The restaurant seats 58 and there's also a conservatory for private parties, small wedding receptions etc. Since opening in 1991 Peter and Sheila Crowland have established a fine reputation for good, home-made food, including numerous unusual dishes, plus an uncommonly good choice of wines and excellent ales, recognised by CAMRA and leading good beer guides. Children are welcome and the Dinosaur Park is nearby. Monthly quiz nights.

YE OLDE HONINGHAM BUCK INN

29 The Street, Honingham, nr Norwich. Tel & Fax: (01603) 880393

Location: village centre.
Credit cards: Mastercard, Visa, Delta, Euro.
Bitters: Greene King Abbot, Flowers Original, Aylesbury Duck.
Lagers: Stella Artois, Carlsberg.

Examples of bar meals (11:30am-3pm, 6:30-10pm - later if nec. - 7 days): *cream cheese & garlic paté; home-cured salmon; devilled lambs' kidneys; steak Diane; chicken with smoked salmon & asparagus; pork & mustard crepes; kleftico; smoked cod & prawn bake; steak & kidney pie; Brancaster mussels; ploughman's; sandwiches; wide selection of vegetarian dishes; daily specials eg warm salad of Norfolk lobster, coronation chicken, seafood specials. Home-made desserts. Children's menu. Trad. Sun. roasts plus alternatives.*

The grape vine has been very active since July '96, when Trevor and Dawn Knibb came to this 14th-century inn (named after John Buck, a notorious smuggler). Customers talk not only of the exceptional food (home-made, even pickles and marmalades) in generous portions (the plates are wide - main course comes with seven vegetables!), but also the personal service - special requests will always be met when possible. This dedication goes for the outside catering service - unusually, all food is cooked on the day (golfers should ask about '19th hole specials'). Joints are roasted the old-fashioned way: on a trivet of vegetables, and chicken, prawns etc are smoked on the premises. There are two pleasant dining rooms, and although one may also eat in the bar, drinkers are always welcome. So are children, and the garden has swings. Dinosaur Park nearby. Really good pianist Friday evenings.

THE ADAM & EVE
Bishopgate, Norwich. Tel: (01603) 667423

Location: behind the cathedral, opposite law courts.
Credit cards: not accepted.
Bitters: Everards Tiger, Theakstons Old Peculier, Adnams, Marstons Pedigree, John Smiths.
Lagers: Kronenbourg, Fosters, Holsten.

Examples of bar meals (12 to 7pm Mon - Sat, 12 to 2:30pm Suns): *cheese & ale soup; trawler pie; Elizabethan pork; chilli; curry; veegtable pie; vegetable bake; shepherds pie; beef & mushroom pie; game pie; turkey & ham pie; fillet of cod or plaice; ham & asparagus rolls with bearnaise sauce; salads; baps; ploughman's; daily specials eg courgette & almond soup, chicken supreme stuffed with apricot sauce & pan-fried aubergines, apple & gooseberry pie. Home-made spicy bread & butter pudding; hot fudge cake; meringue chantilly. Trad. Sun. roasts.*

It's not only the fact that this is the oldest pub (1249) in Norwich which makes it out-of-the-ordinary: it's also the most depicted by photographers and artists and, more to the point, one of the most popular with Norwich people. It's not large and can get very busy (there is a patio to the front for overspill), yet is amazingly well preserved and retains an authentic alehouse atmosphere. Even a sceptic might be tempted to believe that the ghost of Lord Sheffield, hacked to death during Kett's rebellion, still walks the flagstone floors. Colin Burgess has been custodian of this unique legacy over the past 11 years, during which The Adam & Eve has been a regular in the main national guides. Good selection of wines by the glass, and of quality whiskies and brandies. Private parking for 24 plus large public car park opposite.

THE FERRY INN
The Green, Stokesby. Tel: (01493) 751096

Location: riverside, near village green.
Credit cards: not accepted.
Bitters: Adnams, Tolly's, guest.
Lagers: Stella Artois, Heineken.

Examples of bar meals (lunch & evening, 7 days): *pork fillets in sweet & sour sauce; chilli; curry; Norfolk garden pies; steaks; lasagne; fresh Cromer crab; natural plaice in lemon butter sauce; trout; Ferryman's lunch; salads; vegetarian lasagne; 4 daily specials. Cheesecake; fruit pies; gateaux. Children's menu. Trad. Sun. roasts.*

NB: pub closed November to March.

Stokesby is one of Broadland's finest: picturesque, tranquil, unspoilt, all the better for being off the beaten track. The river is probably busier than the road in summer, and many of the boats pull in to this eye-catching 18th-century former cottage, right on the water's edge and rated by Egon Ronay and others. Inside will not disappoint: wooden settles and beams, corner seats and brassware. The cottage origins are most evident in the the large two-tier family lounge, whose concession to the 20th century is a few electronic games in one corner by the entrance. There is a family room, but in kind weather children will want to sit out by the river or head for the play area on the village green. A board on the terrace describes how there was once a ferry across the river.

THE FUR & FEATHER INN
Woodbastwick, nr Norwich. Tel: (01603) 720003

Location: on main road through village.
Credit cards: Mastercard, Visa, Switch, Delta.
Bitters: full Woodfordes range.
Lagers: Heineken, Stella Artois.

Examples of bar/restaurant meals (lunch & evening, 7 days): *chicken & mushroom croissant; chilli dog; ham & mushroom tagliatelle; pork spare ribs; chicken kebabs; meatloaf; Nogin pie; Fur & Feather pie (local game in red wine gravy); Nogin's Yorky; 1/2lb burger topped with prawns; beef teriyaki; veggie burger; cannelloni, spinach & ricotto bake; chestnut & vegetable casserole; steaks; sandwiches; jacket potatoes; salads. Spotted dick; treacle sponge; lemon meringue.*

NB: restaurant open Tues-Sat evenings, bar food every session.

This being the Brewery Tap, the full range of Woodforde's cask-conditioned ales (available in take-home casks), including more than one national 'champion', is dispensed to eager devotees. It has only a few yards to travel from the brewery next door. But this is no mere drinker's den; cleverly converted by John and Jean Marjoram and Woodfordes from 19th-century farm cottages in 1992, one of Norfolk's newer pubs quickly become one of its most popular, not just for the beer but for a surprisingly wide choice of traditional home-made food served in pleasant surroundings. Take time to see the village itself, a throwback to an earlier age, with cottages and a church clustered around a green. Lovely Salhouse Broad is also an easy walk.

THE FISHERMAN'S RETURN

The Lane, Winterton-on-Sea. Tel: (01493) 393305/393631

Location: near village centre and fine sandy beach.
Credit cards: Mastercard, Visa, Switch, Delta.
Accommodation: 3 doubles. £30 single, £50 dbl incl; rooms are quaint with sloping ceilings; tea & coff. facilities; 2 bathrooms, 2 sitting rooms with TV.
Bitters: Scotts Blues & Mild, Theakstons Best, Wolf, Woodfordes Gt Eastern, Mauldons, guest.
Lagers: Holsten, Fosters, Kronenbourg. Plus James White & Scrumpy Jack cider.

Examples of bar meals (lunch & evening 7 days): *fish pie; cottage pie; chilli; omelettes; steaks; roasts; burgers; jacket potatoes; toasted sandwiches; ploughman's; many daily specials eg lentil & vegetable crumble, spiced lamb with lime & coconut, barbecue pork on tagliatelle, vegetable Madras, smoked haddock mornay. Apple & blackberry crumble; lemon & lime cheesecake; double chocolate gateau.*

The windows were once permanently boarded up, as so many bodies were thrown through them when the fishing fleet returned! These days customers usually enter by the door, and find themselves in surprisingly roomy converted 300-year-old fishermen's cottages. To the rear a spacious room for families overlooks a patio and garden with swings and a small menagerie. In winter the open fires broadcast their warm welcome - the winds off the sea are bracing at times. This strange and beautiful coast is a marvellous spot to recharge one's spirits, and for a more prolonged stay there are three charming bedrooms, old fashioned but comfortable. All food is home-cooked to a standard which routinely earns credit from Egon Ronay and other leading guides. Good choice of at least 20 malt whiskies, 22 wines and champagne. Large function room. Dart board.

THE BUTCHER'S ARMS
Oak Lane, East Ruston, nr Stalham. Tel: (01692) 650237 Fax: (01692) 651135

Location: 2 miles inland from Happisburgh lighthouse off the
Bacton to Walcott road.
Credit cards: not accepted.
Bitters: Bass, Adnams, Wadworth 6X, Old Speckled Hen, Tolly
Cobbold Original, Worthington.
Lagers: Carling, Carling Premier.

Examples from lunch menu (7 days): *home-made liver paté; steaks; salads; plough-man's; sandwiches; daily specials eg home-made faggots, barbecue ribs, beef curry, fresh haddock with garlic prawns, black cherry & coconut crumble. Raspberry charlotte russe; lemon & sultana cheesecake; chocolate sin; caramel apple granny. Trad. Sun. roasts.*

Examples from evening menu (7 days): *ham-stuffed peaches; pan-fried pork steak with cider, mushrooms, tarragon & cream sauce; scampi & prawn provencale; curry of the day; vegetable stroganoff; many daily specials eg courgette roulade, five-fish feast, amaretto duck, paella valenciana, California chicken.*

NB: Sunday lunch 12 to 4pm.

A set lunch for just £2 was unbeatable enough seven years ago when first introduced; to have maintained this price to the present day beggars belief, yet there it is, every weekday except Bank Holidays. The secret is that Keith and Margaret Hargrave butcher their own meat, keeping costs down but quality up. Indeed, the centre of what were three 16th-century cottages was once a butcher's shop, hence the name. Now the timbers are bedecked with oddities from the worlds of golf and lacrosse, along with horse brasses. The two restaurants are of quite different character, both very appealing, and may be used for functions. Regular theme evenings in autumn and winter, barbe-cues in summer. Children welcome; nice large garden. Weavers Way weaves its way past here. Coaches welcome.

THE BUCKINGHAMSHIRE ARMS

Blickling Road, Blickling, nr Aylsham. Tel: (01263) 732133

Location: at gates of Blickling Hall.
Credit cards: Mastercard, Visa.
Accommodation: 3 dbls/twins; 1 en-suite, all with 4-posters, TV, tea & coff., hair-dryer, trouser press; £60 per room incl., £50 in winter if dining.
Bitters: Reepham, Adnams, guest.
Lagers: Stella Artois, Carlsberg.

Examples from lunch menu (daily): *potato skins with chilli; chicken/steak & kidney pie; lasagne; casseroles; baguettes; daily specials eg mussel soup with lemon grass & ginger, medallions of pork with apple & grain mustard sauce, salmon supreme with sauté potatoes & chive sauce, jalapino pepper stuffed with cream cheese with capiscum dip. Trad. Sun. roasts £6.50 & £7.50 (2 & 3 courses).*

Examples from evening menu (daily except Sundays): *Thai curry; steaks; smoked haddock with cheese sauce; beef/prawn sizzler; chargrilled chicken & bacon melt; grilled whole lemon sole; vegetarian carbonara; real scampi; daily specials. Lemon & ginger syllabub; treacle tart; creme caramel.*

Given a fresh lease of life by new owners (since June '96) Humble Inns (manager Pip Wilkinson), one of Norfolk's best known and well situated pubs is very much back on the local scene - peak times are very busy. Customers are returning for the modern eclectic cuisine, reasonably priced and served in informal brasserie style. Wine and Gourmet evenings are a regular feature - ask to go on the mailing list. Downstairs has been redecorated, and bedrooms are scheduled for an overhaul, but otherwise this 17th-century inn, built at the same time as the great Hall, remains as it always has been - the original serving hatch can still be seen. Large sheltered garden has 21 tables.

THE SARACEN'S HEAD

Wolterton, nr Erpingham. Tel & Fax: (01263) 768909

Location: adjacent to Wolterton Hall (twixt Erpingham & Itteringham).
Credit cards: Mastercard, Visa, Amex, Switch, Delta.
Accommodation: 3 dbls, 1 twin; all en-suite, TV, hair-dryer, tea & coff; from £35 sngl,
£55 dbl; special breaks from end of Oct to end of March.
Bitters: Adnams, guest.
Lagers: Carlsberg.

Examples of bar meals (lunch & evening, 7 days): *Morston mussels with cider &
cream; paupiettes of bacon & black pudding with tomato sauce; braised duo of wood
pigeon & marsala; medallion of Gunton venison with red fruit; vine leaves stuffed with
goats' cheese, with tomato sauce; large grilled Swaffield trout with parsley butter;
many blackboard specials (revised every session!) eg crispy fried aubergine with
garlic mayonnaise, stockpot soup, salmis of rabbit & smoked ham in honey & mustard,
grilled whole lemon sole. Old fashioned treacle tart; chocolate & orange cheesecake;
brown bread & butter pudding. Trad. Sun. roasts.*

NB: special 2-course weekday lunch £4.95, Sunday supper £5.95.

"Norfolk Dining Pub of the Year" (Good Pub Guide) for three of the past four years,
highly rated by other leading guides and enormously popular locally, this
individualistic eating house has put Wolterton on the gastronomic map, if not most
road maps. The building itself is engagingly eccentric, modelled on a Tuscan
farmhouse with a lovely courtyard to the rear. The sense of utter tranquility yields to
live jazz or flamenco on Sunday evenings, and there is a full programme of events
throughout the year. Chef proprietor Robert Dawson-Smith likes to inject a little
humour into a very civilised and welcoming atmosphere, not disturbed by piped
music. Great views from comfortable bedrooms. Upstairs function room for 54.

THE THREE SWALLOWS
Newgate Green, Cley-next-the-Sea. Tel: (01263) 740526

Location: on village green near church, 1/2 mile off coast road towards Holt.
Credit cards: not accepted.
Accommodation: 5 dbls/twins, 1 family, all en-suite; £19.50pp in summer,
£14 in winter, incl. Eng. breakfast.
Bitters: Greene King, Tetley, Kilkenny.
Lagers: Stella Artois.

Examples of bar meals (lunch & evening, 7 days): *home-made lasagne; steaks; whole prawns in garlic butter; cod; salads; rolls & sandwiches; daily specials eg home-made steak & kidney pie, local mussels in cream sauce, mixed grill, crab salad, Cajun chicken breast, broccoli & stilton quiche. Treacle tart; apple pie; hot chocolate fudge cake. Trad. Sun. roasts.*

It's hard to believe, but Cley was once a large and bustling port. The harbour was directly opposite this 17th-century sailors' inn - the mooring rings can still be seen - but now is a narrow river in open meadows. This peaceful prospect is just one of the pleasures of an unpretentious and homely rural retreat, whose cottage origins are evident in the long, narrow bar, warmed by open coal fires. Dozens of old photos may engage your interest, but of particular note is the ornately carved bar counter. Children are welcome, and the lovely one-acre garden is home to four goats and an aviary. The bedrooms, with their polished wood floors and small sofas, are incredibly good value, especially in such a choice location. The home-made food is also modestly priced.

THE WHITE HORSE HOTEL & FREEHOUSE
4 High Street, Blakeney. Tel: (01263) 740574

Location: village centre.
Credit cards: Mastercard, Visa, Amex.
Accommodation: 2 singles, 4 doubles, 1 twin, 2 family, all en suite bathrooms, TV's, tea & coff; from £30 pp incl; special rates for children and winter breaks.
Bitters: Adnams, Boddingtons, Flowers.
Lagers: Stella Artois, Heineken.

Examples of bar meals (lunch & evening, 7 days): *deep fried herring roes on toast; local whitebait; mussels; fisherman's pie; sirloin steak; local crabs; vegetarian dishes; daily specials eg homemade steak & kidney pudding, tagliatelle with smoked salmon & broccoli sauce, mushroom & stilton pancakes. Spotted dick; treacle tart; bread & butter pudding.*

Examples of restaurant meals (evenings Tues - Sat; booking advised weekends): *chargrilled breast of pigeon with braised turnip & black pudding; poached garden pears with stilton & walnut mousse; grilled fillets of red mullet with spring onion & basil sauce; ballantine of chicken with crab sauce; roast fillet of lamb with sesame & herb crust on red wine sauce. Iced terrine of nougatine with raspberry sauce; grilled pear with hot chocolate sauce & honey & ginger ice cream.*

What a place for a weekend break - the views over the quay from some of the warm, very well appointed bedrooms are superb. The intimate little restaurant (converted from stables) overlooking the attractive walled courtyard has acquired a sterling reputation for good food, accompanied by an excellent wine list. Chef Chris Hyde (formerly of Regatta, Aldeburgh) relies heavily on fresh and mostly local produce, especially seafood. But if your fancy is simply a good pint and maybe a hearty bar meal, this freehouse is also eminently suitable. Residents car park in front of hotel. No dogs.

THE KING'S ARMS HOTEL FREEHOUSE
Westgate Street, Blakeney Tel. (01263) 740341

Location: near quayside, west end of village.
Credit cards: Mastercard, Visa, Switch.
Accommodation: 5 dbls/twins, all en-suite, TV; all but one with outstanding views over Blakeney Point; plus self- contained holiday flatlets; £55 per room in summer, from £40 winter, incl. breakfast; special breaks & weekly rates.
Bitters: Woodfordes, Webster, Ruddles, Marston's Pedigree, guests.
Lagers: Fosters, Carlsberg, Holsten.

Examples of bar meals (ALL DAY & EVERY DAY; winter weekdays may vary but food ALWAYS available all day at weekends): *home-made pies; seafood pasta; local crabs; mussels; prawns; salads; vegetarian dishes; steaks; fresh fish local trout; salmon; daily specials eg steak & kidney pie, chilli, game pie, filled Yorkshire puds, tuna & pasta bake, spaghetti bolognese. Bread pudding; fruit crumbles; treacle sponge.*

NB OPEN ALL DAY, EVERY DAY

Blakeney would be many people's choice for East Anglia's most picturesque village. Its flint cottages, alleys and courtyards are a delight on the eye, and the views over the marshes provide a lovely backdrop. Just off the quayside (from which there are regular seal trips in season), The King's Arms was once three narrow fishermen's cottages, but is now one of the most popular pubs in the area, recommended by national guides. Licensees Howard and Marjorie Davies left the world of the Black and White Minstrels and My Fair Lady 25 years ago. They welcome children and even dogs if the bar is not full (which in summer it usually is, but there is a garden with swings). Even smokers may appreciate the facility of a no-smoking area in a tasteful new extension, to better enjoy the good food. See if you can spot the 1953 flood tide mark on an inside wall. No piped music or jukebox.

169

THE CHEQUERS INN

Front Street, Binham, nr Fakenham. Tel: (01328) 830297

Location: village centre, on B1388 between Wells and Walsingham.
Credit cards: Mastercard, Visa, Delta, Switch, JCB - surcharge of £1 on all credit card or cheque transactions.
Accommodation: Single £22, dbl £36, family £40 per room incl. TV's, tea & coff; WHB & shaving point; bathroom adjacent.
Bitters: Adnams Best, Greene King Abbot & IPA, Bass, Toby, guests. Plus Mitchell & Butler's Mild.
Lagers: Carling, Carling Premier, Tennents Extra.

Examples of bar meals (12-2pm daily, 6-9pm Mon-Sat, 6-7pm Suns): *fresh home-made soups; crispy Thai-style king prawns; steak & kidney pie; spinach, mushroom & tomato lasagne; steaks & grills; salmon mornay; trout stuffed with prawns & asparagus in white wine sauce; quail stuffed with red rice, apricots & raisins in madeira sauce; salads; jacket potatoes; sandwiches; daily specials eg home-made pies, fresh local crab, chicken satay. Black Forest gateau; sponge puddings; fruit pies. Trad. Sun. roasts £6.25 (2 courses), 12 - 2pm.*

NB: open 11:30am to 3pm, 5:30pm to 11pm Mon - Sat; 12 to 3pm, 7 to 10:30pm Sundays.

One of Norfolk's finest villages, famed for its ancient priory, Binham is also blessed with one of the county's foremost freehouses, standing in one acre in the village centre. Unusual in that the freehold is held in a charitable trust belonging to the village, the charming 17th-century Chequers has since Jan. '91 been run by current proprietors Brian Pennington and Barbara Garratt. Having gained an enviable reputation for fine food and ales and wines, Brian and Barbara make full use of their culinary skills and the best of fresh local produce to present quality dishes at value-for-money prices. The bar itself oozes character, with its exposed beams and open fires; of special interest is an engraving of the Battle of Portsmouth, during which the Mary Rose sunk. Well behaved children welcome. Large beer garden. No-smoking area. Handy for all the attractions of this lovely area.

THE THREE HORSESHOES
Warham, nr Wells-next-Sea. Tel: (01328) 710547

Location: village centre.
Credit cards: under review.
Accommodation: 1 single, 2 doubles (1 en suite), + 2 s/c cottages in N.Creake.
Bitters: Woodfordes, Greene King, guests.
Lagers: Carlsberg. Plus home-made lemonade and award-winning
Whin Hill cider from Wells

Examples of bar/dining room meals (lunch & evening, 7 days): *smokie hotpot; game terrine; potted cheese & port; potted smoked fish; cheesy mushroom bake; haddock fillet in cheese sauce; fisherman's pie; chicken & rabbit pie; steak & beer pie; venison pie; orchard pork pie; lamb & tomato pie; cheesy vegetable pie; mushroom, walnut & wine pie; braised sirloin in tomato sauce; plaice in seafood sauce; courgette, tomato & cheese bake; liver & onions. Nelson cake; spotted dick; pear upside-down pudding; apricot & rum sponge.*

This genuinely unspoilt 18th-century cottage pub will evoke memories of a less frantic age. It's totally 'un-modern', to the extent of a 1940's fruit machine in one corner. Bare floors, open fires, old furniture and gas lighting complete the agreeable illusion. One recent concession to modernity is the brand new toilet block for the disabled. What was the children's room is now a lounge, but families are still welcome, and the garden borders a stream and the village green. Seafood is the house speciality, but the menu includes many meat and vegetarian alternatives, all at very modest prices. Also good value is the accommodation, in a picturebook cottage with roses round the door and working water pump in the garden - an idyllic rural retreat in a timeless flint village.

THE STIFFKEY RED LION
44 Wells Road, Stiffkey, nr Wells. Tel: (01328) 830552 Fax: (01328) 855983

Location: on A149 coast road, 1 mile from marshes & coastal path.
Credit cards: Mastercard, Visa, Switch, Delta.
Bitters: Woodfordes (from the barrel), other East Anglian guests.
Lagers: Stella Artois, Carlsberg.

Examples of bar meals (lunch & evening, 7 days): *pan-fried liver & bacon with bubble & squeak; steak & kidney pie; roast chicken in tarragon sauce; local crab & mussels; vegetarian dishes; fresh baguettes with various fillings. Sponge puddings; treacle tart; spotted dick; summer pudding; strawberries & cream; local ice cream. Trad. Sun. roast.*

Stiffkey achieved notoriety through its erstwhile vicar, who wanted to save loose women and ended in the jaws of a lion. Being 16th-century, this Red Lion was there long before him, and would seem to have a piano-playing ghost who is given to moving barstools about! It's now the only pub left in one of Norfolk's most picturesque flint villages, but fortunately is one well worth stopping off for. With four open fires, stripped wood and tiled floors, old wooden settles and traditional pub games, the bar is simple and authentic. To the rear are a smart conservatory and dining room. Functions up to 40 are catered for, and outside bars and wedding receptions are gladly arranged. The management is keen on hospitality, and does welcome children. Service is as speedy as possible given that all is fresh and cooked to order (local produce favoured). Terrace overlooks lovely river valley. Large car park.

THE HOSTE ARMS
The Green, Burnham Market. Tel: (01328) 738777 Fax: (01328) 730103

Location: village centre.
Credit cards: Mastercard, Visa, Switch.
Accommodation: 15 dbls/twins, 1 family, 4 suites; all en-suite, TV, phone, hair-dryer,
tea & coff; £60 sngl, £86 dbl; Nov - March midweek breaks;
weekend breaks throughout the year.
Bitters: Greene King IPA & Abbot, Woodfordes Wherry.
Lagers: Fosters, Kronenbourg.

Examples of bar/restaurant meals (lunch & evening, 7 days): *assiette of sushi with accompaniments; rocket & french bean salad with black pudding & chorizo sausage; pan-fried collops of monkfish, braised fennel in tomato with dauphinoise potato; best end of English lamb with wild mushrooms & beetroot compote; gateau of aubergine, goats' cheese & plum tomato with pimento dressing. Individual apricot & coconut frangipane tart with orange cream sauce; chocolate & pistachio terrine. Trad. Sun. roasts.*

Under Paul Whittome's energetic direction since 1989, 'The Hoste' (managed by Rebecca McKenzie) has emerged as one of the most talked about inns in the entire country, reaping a hatful of awards, including 'Inn of the Year 1996' from both Egon Ronay and Johanssen, and most recently Good Hotels Guide 'Inn of the Year'. The foundation of this amazing success is the diverse international menu (chef Stephen David), but the splendid bedrooms are also much in demand (the old railway station just up the road has recently been annexed and converted to provide extra, very peaceful accommodation). Nelson, who was born nearby, doubtless supped at this handsome 17th-century inn, named after one of his captains; one wonders what he would make of the live jazz on the first Friday of each month. Upstairs a gallery features a monthly guest artist, but if even all this can't keep you here, Jeanne Whittome runs a travel agency!

THE LIFEBOAT INN

Ship Lane, Thornham, nr Hunstanton. Tel: (01485) 512236Fax: (01485) 512323

Location: on a loop off A149 (signposted), overlooking harbour to sea.
Credit cards: Mastercard, Visa, Switch, Eurocard, Delta.
Accommodation: 13 dbls/twins; all en-suite, TV, phone, hair- dryer, tea & coff.
EATB 3 Crowns; from £30pp; special midweek & weekend breaks;
most rooms have panoramic views.
Bitters: Adnams, Woodfordes Wherry, Greene King, guests.
Lagers: Tennents, Carling. Plus Westons Scrumpy cider.

Examples of bar meals (lunch & evening, 7 days): *crab & ginger filo parcels; Lifeboat fish pie; breast of chicken stuffed with honey ham & fresh spinach on bed of mange tout; steaks; trad. fish & chips; ragout of Mediterranean vegetables; salads; open sandwiches; ploughman's. Thornham mud pie; hot apple & sultana crumble; lemon curd bread & butter pudding. Children's menu.*

Examples of restaurant meals (as above): *gateau of black pudding, apple & mortadella with Calvados cream sauce; whole roasted Thornham sea bass with tomato & chive butter sauce; medallions of lamb topped with melted chaumes centred with pickled walnuts; brown nut rissoles. Trad. Sun. roasts. Afternoon teas.*

Little changed since the 15th century (the Smugglers' Bar is still lit by hanging oil lamps), this former smugglers' alehouse is one of England's 'Classic Inns', in a unique location commanding stunning views to the sea. Proprietors since June '95, Charles and Angie Coker are more than keen to safeguard the very special character of the place. This respect for tradition extends to the kitchen, where "catch of the day" local game and seafood is the house speciality. You may not need a lunch after one of their breakfasts! Guitarist often performs Friday evenings. Children, dogs and muddy boots welcome! **Special offer: 2 nights for the price of 1 from Nov - March (midweek only, excl. holidays and subject to availibility) with this guide.**

THE WHITE HORSE
Kirkgate Street, Holme-next-the-Sea. Tel: (01485) 525512

Location: just off A149, at end of Peddars Way.
Credit cards: not accepted.
Bitters: Bass, Flowers Original, Boddington, Worthington, occasional guest.
Lagers: Stella Artois, Carling.

Examples of bar/dining room meals (lunch & evening daily except Sun evenings and all day Mons): *torpedo prawns in crispy crumb; hot jalapeno peppers filled with cream cheese; crab salad; steaks; ploughman's; blackboard specials eg whale-sized cod in batter (noted), honeyroast duck in orange sauce, fresh poached salmon, vegetable samosas; raspberry & hazelnut roulade. Black Forest Alaska; death by white chocolate; treacle pud; spotted dick; banoffi banoffi. Trad. Sun. roasts in winter.*

This exquisite little village marks the end of the Peddars Way. In the distant past it was the ferry across The Wash which brought travellers here; now they beat a path for fresh, home-cooked food, but most especially for the fabled fish and chips, at this early- 17th-century farmhouse. It has been run by the same family for 54 years - a personal attachment unimaginable to the trendy executives who are ruining so many other fine pubs. The uneven floor may have you convinced you've had one too many, and three chairs may be one too many in the secretive little 'Acorn Nooky'. But it is the feature inglenook which catches the eye in a lovely dining room; actually it's three rooms in one. Children are welcome there or in the large beer garden. Superb beaches, golf, riding, Sandringham and Holkham are all close by.

THE GOLDEN LION HOTEL
The Green, Hunstanton. Tel: (01485) 532688 Fax: (01485) 535310

Location: town centre, on green overlooking sea.
Credit cards: Mastercard, Visa, Diners, Switch, Delta.
Accommodation: 18 dbls; all en-suite, TV, phone, hair-dryer, tea & coff; all with sea views; one ground floor suite for disabled; from £54 sngl, £69 dbl; ask about special breaks.
Bitters: Greene King, Bass, guest.
Lagers: Kronenbourg, Harp Irish, Carlsberg Premium.

Examples of bar meals (12 to 3:30pm, 6:30 to 9pm - 9:30 Sats - 7 days): *home-made lasagne; steak & ale pie; broccoli bake; steaks; baguettes; salads; sandwiches; daily specials eg sweet & sour beef stir-fry, grilled halibut in lemon butter, fishcakes. Dutch apple crumble; banoffee pie; lemon lush. Senior Citizens' lunch £4.50.*

Examples of restaurant meals (daily, evenings only): *deep-fried brie with apricot glaze; king prawns sautéed in garlic butter & white wine. Chicken supreme filled with spinach & cheese, served with stilton & apple sauce; fillet steak Normandy; baked Dover sole with creamy mushroom sauce.*

NB: bar open 11am to 11pm (12 to 10:30pm Sundays).

After years of shameful neglect, Hunstanton's first and finest building (1846) has been restored to full glory, top to bottom. Always in a premier position, it is once again a premier seaside hotel in the most honourable tradition, managed by Colin Rushmore (36 years in the business). From the terraced garden in summer you could watch the sun set in the sea and rise from it again a few hours later - not many places you can do that. In between enjoy fresh, home-made cooking (sometimes on a weekly theme, like French or Italian), take in a cabaret or 60s Night, and maybe stay in one of the very spacious, well appointed bedrooms. Great venue for weddings, conferences etc.

THE GIN TRAP INN

High Street, Ringstead, nr Hunstanton. Tel: (01485) 525264

Location: village centre.
Credit cards: not accepted.
Bitters: Greene King, Charrington, Worthington, Adnams, Toby,
Gin Trap Own,Woodfordes, guests.
Lagers: Carling, Tennents, Tennents L.A.

Examples of bar meals (lunch & evening, 7 days): *home-made lasagne; steak & kidney pie (not in brown bowl); steaks; freshly cut ham; chicken Kiev; chicken with leek & stilton; home-made quiches; toad-in-the-hole; scampi; plaice; nut cutlets.; daily specials eg h/m mushroom & sherry soup, fresh fish & chips, Home-made bread & butter pudding; treacle pud; fruit crumbles; chocolate brandy crunch cake; sponge puds.* Lunchtimes only: *jacket potatoes; ploughman's; sandwiches. Children's menu. Trad. Sun. roasts average £5.75.*

"25lb dragon steaks with dwarf beans are available on 30th February, price £400.00" After a few pints of Gin Trap bitter you may feel tempted to tackle this most unlikely entry on the menu, but portions of more conventional fare are in truth generous, though prices somewhat more modest. Since acquiring this 17th-century coaching inn in 1987, Margaret and Brian Harmes have made this one of the area's most popular pubs, a favourite watering hole of ramblers, who are politely requested to remove muddy boots before walking on the monogrammed carpet! Countless gin traps have been cleverly adapted as light fittings, and rural implements of all kinds cover the ceiling. There are two car parks, one of which has stocks where miscreants were once pelted. Why not combine your visit with a look at the adjacent country and sporting art gallery? Walled beer garden. Occasional visits from Morris dancers, and regular entertainment at the piano.

THE ROSE & CROWN

Old Church Road, Snettisham. Tel: (01485) 541382 Fax: (01485) 543172

Location: near church.
Credit cards: Mastercard, Visa, Switch.
Accommodation: 5 dbls/twins, £30 pp; all en suite, TV, hair dryer, tea & coff.
Oct - March winter breaks.
Bitters: Adnams, Bass, Woodfordes, Shepherd Neame, guests.
Lagers: Carling, Carling Premier, Tennents Extra.

Examples of bar/restaurant meals (lunch & evening, 7 days): *fresh local mussels in garlic & white wine sauce; home-made country paté; steak & kidney pie (noted); Armenian lamb; steaks; chicken curry; Thai stir-fry; bangers & mash; seared cod on bed of spinach with chive butter sauce; vegetable chilli; fresh-baked baguettes (lunch only); salads, many daily specials eg seafood beignets with fish cream sauce, duck breast with orange sauce, rack of lamb with rosemary sauce. Home-made apple crumble, bread & butter pudding, fresh fruit pavlova, pecan & maple syrup tart. Children's menu. Trad. Sun. roasts £5.95 (1 course).*

This is a country pub which seems to have everything: situated in a lovely corner of the region (near to Sandringham, Norfolk Lavender, Castle Rising and some marvellous beaches); the character of a 14th-century freehouse (old timbers, magnificent open fireplaces, a Public Bar with barrel seats); quality bedrooms at a reasonable price; an outstanding play area with an aviary and rabbits in a pretty, sheltered garden; a large Garden Room, ideal for wedding receptions and other functions. If this were not enough, food is of a very high order, portions generous and served by friendly staff. Hence the inn has won many awards, and is starred in all the main national guides. A programme of quizzes and entertainment includes live music alternate Thursday evenings.

THE KING'S HEAD HOTEL

Gt Bircham, nr King's Lynn. Tel: (01485) 578265

Location: village centre, on B1153.
Credit cards: Mastercard, Visa.
Accommodation: 2 dbls, 3 twins, all en-suite, TV; £59 per room; dinner, b & b £65 - £75.
Bitters: Adnams, Bass.
Lagers: Carling, Tennents Extra.

Examples of bar meals (lunch & evening, 7 days): *chicken cacciatore; lasagne; curries; steak & kidney pudding; salads; ploughman's. Chocolate & Grand Marnier cheesecake; apple, rhubarb & ginger pie; banoffee pie; mocha Katie; bread & butter pudding; strawberry & apricot tart.*

Examples of restaurant meals (as above): *fillet of halibut in prawn & garlic sauce; breast of duck in mango sauce; sirloin pizzaola; fresh pasta dishes; daily specisl eg cheese & vegetable bake; fishcakes with crab sauce, whole lobster. Trad. Sun. roasts.*

The Royal Sandringham Estate, to which the hotel once belonged, draws thousands of visitors to this lovely part of Norfolk. Birdwatchers, yachtsmen and all lovers of gentle, rolling countryside will find spiritual sustenance in unspoilt nature. Sustenance of a more material kind is the speciality of The King's Head, where food is served in all three bars and the rather pretty restaurant. The last Friday of each month is Italian Night, although Italian dishes are always on the menu. The proprietor is himself Italian, so naturally children are welcome, and they have their own room - there's also a large garden (and car park). Historic King's Lynn and Houghton Hall are very close, so one is well placed for a protracted stay.

THE FFOLKES ARMS HOTEL & COUNTRY CLUB
Hillington, nr King's Lynn. Tel: (01485) 600210 Fax: (01485) 601196

Location: on A148.
Credit cards: Mastercard, Visa, Amex, Switch, Delta.
Accommodation: 18 dbls/twins, 2 family; all recently refurbished, en-suite, TV, hair-dryer, trouser press, tea & coff; £35 sngl, £50 dbl; midweek breaks 3 nights £33pp per night incl. 3-course carvery.
Bitters: Bass, Worthington, Adnams.
Lagers: Tennents, Tennents Extra, Carling, Staropramen.

Examples of bar meals (lunch & evening, 7 days): *deep-fried potato skins with cheese & ham filling; hot peppered mackerel; home-made steak & ale pie; lasagne; chilli; pasta speciality; steaks & grills; vegetarian dishes; baguettes; ploughman's; salads; roast of the day. OAP specials.*

Examples of restaurant meals (as above): *melon tropicana; crevettes in garlic butter. Ffolkes special chicken; poached salmon with white wine, prawns & cream sauce; medallions of beef stilton; aubergine bake; daily carvery; 'Gourmet Board'. Good selection of home-made desserts eg tiramisu, cheesecakes, fruit pies & gateaux.*

This former simple coaching inn has evolved under Monica and Lawrence Bates over the past 16 years into a leisure and business complex. Not only has the original building been greatly extended, 20 tastefully furnished bedrooms occupy the site of the old stable block, and now a Country Club has been added, with snooker and pool tables, championship dartboards, satellite TV and a fully equipped function room (ideal for wedding receptions). Live entertainment is laid on some weekends. This amazing success story has been built on value for money, home-cooked food, amiable staff and the personal touch. Well placed for Hunstanton, Sandringham, Houghton Hall, Thursford and much else.

THE ROSE & CROWN

Nethergate Street, Harpley, nr Fakenham. Tel: (01485) 520577

Location: off A148 King's Lynn to Fakenham road (opp. Houghton Hall turn-off).
Credit cards: not accepted.
Bitters: Greene King, Tetley.
Lagers: Stella Artois, Heineken.

Examples of bar meals (lunch & evening, 7 days): *mushrooms in garlic butter; Crown smokie; seafood parcels with plum dip; chicken, broccoli & stilton pie; chicken Madras; aromatic lamb with apricots; pork casserole with apples, sage & cider; steaks; steak & kidney pie; vegetarian chilli; pizzas; ploughman's; daily specials eg ostrich steaks, smitten steak, Cromer crab salad. Home-made apple flan; syrup tart; warm chocolate fudge cake; poached pears in red wine. Children's menu. Trad. Sun. roasts (booking advised).*

This attractive 17th-century pub is waiting to be discovered just a few seconds' drive off the busy A148, in one of the loveliest parts of the region, near to Peddars Way and Sandringham and adjacent to the turning for Houghton Hall. Under the stewardship of Michael and Liz Kentfield since spring '89, it is popular with locals, walkers and visitors alike - families are especially welcome. The sizable menu, supplemented by daily specials, is a blend of traditional favourites with a little overseas influence to add zest. The home cooking may be enjoyed in bar or separate dining room. Pool, darts dominoes and crib are the indoor amusements, outside there's an enclosed garden with play area and occasional barbecues. Michael and Liz also run a successful outside catering service, and can put you in contact with excellent bed & breakfast accommodation in the village.

THE BOAR INN

Gt Ryburgh, nr Fakenham. Tel: (01328) 829212

Location: end of village, opp. 13th-century church.
Credit cards: Mastercard, Visa, Connect.
Accommodation: 1 single (£25 per night, £120 per week), 3 dbls/twins (£45 per night,
£190 per week, maybe let at single rate), 1 family; all en-suite.
Bitters: Wensum (own brand), Adnams, Greene King, Burtons, Tetley, Kilkenny.
Lagers: Carlsberg, Lowenbrau.

Examples of bar/restaurant meals (lunch & evening, 7 days): *mushroom royale (cooked with stilton & garlic); lasagne; steak & kidney pie; Madras beef curry; salads; steaks; chicken cordon bleu; barbecue lamb cutlets; salmon steak in mushroom & cream sauce; veal cusiniere (with apple, orange brandy sauce & cream); chicken tikka; steaks; lemon sole with prawns; courgette & pasta bake; daily specials eg chicken & bacon carbonara. Italian ices; meringue glacé; fruit crumble.*

With newly refurbished bedrooms (scheduled for Jan '98), The Boar makes for a marvellous rural retreat in the heart of the county, ideal for an extended visit (and perhaps for a hair-do at the salon on the premises!). But it is principally the food which earns the regular listing in major national guides. All is cooked to order, so allow a little extra time to be served at peak periods. A short stroll to the clear River Wensum, which meanders through a meadow just yards to the rear of the shaded, rose-scented garden (the patio is a sun trap) would fill the time nicely; or take the opportunity to look around this ancient inn - the cosy beamed bar is warmed by an open fire in winter, and the dining room is also very attractive and spacious. Just across the road is an excellent example of the country church for which Norfolk is famed.

THE CROWN
Colkirk, nr Fakenham. Tel: (01328) 862172

Location: village centre.
Credit cards: Mastercard, Visa.
Bitters: Greene King IPA & Abbot, Rayments Special, Wexford. Plus Mild.
Lagers: Carling, Kronenbourg.

Examples of bar meals (lunch & evening, 7 days): *gratin of mushrooms & prawns; mushroom, ham & leek cheesy bake; cheesy cottage pie; local crab salad; steak & kidney pie; duck liver & armagnac paté; hot Thai chicken; home-made soups; fresh fish of the day; prime Scotch steaks; casseroles; curries; min. 6 veg. choices eg creamy vegetable pancakes; daily specials eg tomato & mozarella salad in basil vinaigrette, tiger prawns in hot oriental sauce, fresh halibut fillet in white wine sauce, fresh battered cod, kidneys in red wine gravy. Homemade hot puddings; gateaux; cheese-cake; extensive cheeseboard. Trad. Sun roasts.*

Folk in these parts seem to be unanimous in praise of their local, and it is hard to find fault with such an honest example of the English country pub at its best. The food is fresh and home cooked, the bar and dining room comfortable and pleasant, and the atmosphere congenial. Traditional games like skittles, shove ha'penny, darts and dominoes provide amusement. In winter, warm the extremities with a good hot meal by an open fire; in summer do the same in the sun on the patio or in the beer garden (formerly a bowling green), perhaps with a bottle of wine from a an extensive, personally selected list, all available by the glass - The Crown is noted as one of the top five wine pubs in the country. Pat and Rosemary Whitmore are your amicable hosts, well established here over many years.

THE GREAT DANE'S HEAD
The Green, Beachamwell, nr Swaffham. Tel: (01366) 328443

Location: on village green, opp. church.
Credit cards: not acepted.
   Bitters: Greene King Abbot, IPA, guest.
   Lagers: Harp, Kronenbourg.

Examples of bar/restaurant meals (12 - 2:30pm, 7 -10pm, 7 days): *home-made steak & kidney pie; game pie; turkey & stilton pie; noisettes of lamb; steaks; traditional paella; traditional paella; chicken Wellington; spicy beef; seafood parcel; seafood tagliatelle; sweet & sour prawns; wing of skate; trout; game in season.*

The three pub signs will bewilder the unwary: one shows the head of a large dog; another that of a Viking; a third tells us this is 'The Hole in the Wall'. It was in fact once known as The Cooper's Arms, but as there was no bar beer was served through a hole in the wall. Well, this is Norfolk. And Beachamwell is one of the county's many secrets, for it's a lovely, unspoilt village in the middle of nowhere, distinguished by the only thatched church with a round tower in Norfolk - it's very, very old. The pub commands a perfect view of it over the classic village green. Built around 1820 (although the cellar is older), it has been refurbished by Frank and Jenny White, who have made it very popular for good, homecooked food in generous portions at reasonable prices. Staple favourites rub shoulders with the exotic, augmented by theme nights such as Thai. One can sit in the garden in summer. B & B in village.

THE HARE ARMS

Stow Bardolph, nr Downham Market. Tel: (01366) 382229 Fax: (01366) 385522

Location: off A10 between King's Lynn (9 miles) and Downham Market (2 miles).
Credit cards: Mastercard, Visa, Switch, Delta.
Bitters: Greene King.
Lagers: Kronenbourg, Harp.

Examples of bar meals (lunch & evening daily): *fresh fish daily eg rolled plaice fillet filled with spinach & tomato concasse in white wine cream sauce; home-made chilli; curry; lasagne; steaks; salads; sandwiches; daily specials eg skate wing in lemon butter sauce, pork steak in apricot sauce, spicy mixed bean bake with leek & cheese topping. Children's menu. Bar food served in restaurant Sunday lunchtimes.*

Examples of restaurant meals (a la carte Mon - Sat evenings, bookings advised): *paté profiteroles; lemon sole florentine; sea bass in paper parcel in white wine & julienne of vegetables; saffron chicken breast in spices with sauce of marinade & creme fraiche; beef smitan. Home-made fruit-filled meringue nests; hot pecan pie; chocolate torte. Also table d'hote (£16.75) Mon-Thurs evenings. Trad. Sun. roast.*

21 years under the same ownership, this popular ivy-clad inn in a pleasant little village has been recommended by Egon Ronay 16 years running for the delicious wholesome fare, and was also named Regional Pub of the Year 1993 in the Eastern Daily Press. Fresh local produce is used whenever possible - crab and lobster in summer, pheasant, pigeon and game in winter. The high-standard restaurant, a beautifully proportioned room, offers a menu of traditional and international dishes changed frequently. The 'Old Coach House' is available for a variety of functions, from private dinner or office parties to weddings (and family use on Sundays). Families are also welcome in the roomy conservatory or attractive garden. NATIONAL WINNER OF 'PUB CATERER OF THE YEAR' AWARD 1997.

THE JENYNS ARMS

Denver Sluice, nr Downham Market. Tel & Fax: (01366) 383366

Location: riverside, about 2 miles south-west of Downham Market.
Credit cards: Mastercard, Visa.
Accommodation: 4 dbls/twins, 1 family, in chalets; all en-suite, TV, hair-dryer, tea & coff.
Bitters: Greene King, Adnams, Boddingtons, Flowers, guest
(always one on special offer).
Lagers: Grolsch, Tennents, Carling, Kronenbourg.

Examples of bar/dining room meals (lunch & evening, except Sun. evening): *spare ribs; lasagne; chilli; curries; vegetarian dish of the day; whole king prawns in garlic; salads; jacket potatoes; sandwiches; chicken breast stuffed with paté in red wine & mushroom sauce; steaks & grills; fresh fish; many daily specials eg broccoli & mushroom bake, steak & mushroom pie, duck a l'orange. Homemade sweets. Children's menu. Trad. Sun. roasts.*

Clive and Karen Hughes, licensees for over nine years, could be forgiven for relying on the marvellous location, right by a broad expanse of navigable river, to draw custom, but their 100-year-old pub would be well worth the diversion wherever situated. Approached by a narrow, bumpy lane (leading from opposite the church in Denver village), it stands in splendid isolation in the flat, watery Fenland landscape. A tollboard outside reminds us that it once cost one penny to cross the river! Inside, one's gaze is drawn to that incredible view; the conservatory is the place to be in winter, and you may spot peacocks in the riverside garden in summer. They don't appear on the menu, of course, but much else does, including fish fresh from Grimsby and meat from the local butcher. The function room takes up to 60; a dream for wedding photographers. Children welcome. Darts. Discos Sunday evenings. Recommended by national guides.

THE RED LION
32 North Brink, Wisbech. Tel: (01945) 582022

Location: north bank of River Nene, near town centre.
Credit cards: Mastercard, Visa, Switch, Delta.
Bitters: Elgoods Cambridge & Pageant, guests.
Lagers: Carlsberg, Carlsberg Export, Konig.

Examples of bar/restaurant meals (lunch & evening, 7 days): *bacon & onion pudding; all-day breakfast; chicken strips pan-fried in creamy stilton & mushroom sauce; stilton & vegetable bake; steaks & grills; lemon sole with crabmeat; seafood medley; Cantonese prawns; trout fillet with almond breadcrumbs; salmon fillet with creamy prawn & dill sauce; home-baked filled rolls (lunch only); daily specials eg liver & bacon casserole, cottage pie; lasagne. Raspberry & yoghurt surprise; apple, cinammon & sultana pie; spotted dick; cherry flan; sticky toffee pudding. Trad. Sun. roasts.*

The much-photographed parade of handsome Georgian buildings along the riverbank is so redolent of Holland, but at its centre this former coaching inn is firmly rooted in English tradition. Unpretentious and comfortable, with a laid-back atmosphere, it has a long, timbered bar, bench seating and barrels set in the wall and bar counter. Only 400 yards from the Elgood Brewery (open to visitors), it might be called the brewery tap. It was once owned by the illustrious Peckover family, and lovely Peckover Hall and its famous garden are only yards away. Richard Cropley became landlord in November '96 (after nearly four years as manager), and chalks up a daily blackboard menu of good, traditional home cooking- even the rolls are home-baked. Children welcome in dining room and small patio. Piped music. Parking to rear and on road.

THE MILLSTONE INN
Millstone Lane, Barnack, nr Stamford.   Tel & Fax: (01780) 740296

Location: village centre.
Credit cards: Mastercard, Visa, Switch, Delta.
Bitters: Everards Tiger, Old Original, Adnams Southwold, 2 guests.
Lagers: Stella Artois, Carling.

Examples of bar meals (lunch & evening daily except Sun. evenings): *home-made pies (speciality) eg chicken & prawn, steak & ale; leek & mushroom crepe; stilton chicken; deep-fried cod; steaks & grills; ploughman's; sandwiches; daily specials eg smoked haddock & bacon mornay, lamb navarin, fish pie, cottage pie. Home-made chocolate cheesecake; strawberry shortcake; fruit pies & crumbles; lemon brulée; bread & butter pudding; chocolate & orange trifle; treacle sponge. Children's menu. Trad. Sun. roasts plus alternatives.*

The mellow stone villages in this area call to mind the Cotswolds. Barnack is one of the prettiest, and is also graced with one of the best pubs in the area for food and ale, as acknowledged by major national guides. The three bar areas are warm and hospitable, but sun lovers may prefer the walled patio. Landlord (for over 13 years) Aubrey Sinclair-Ball is pleased to welcome youngsters; he describes the restaurant as a family one, and there's also a children's room with games and video. For the grown-ups there are live jazz evenings and the occasional karaoke and disco nights. Stamford, one of England's finest towns, is very near, as are Burghley House and Hill Hole stone quarry with rare flowers.

THE CROWN INN
Duck Street, Elton, nr Peterborough. Tel: (01832) 280232

Location: lower village - follow signs for Nassington off A605.
Credit cards: Mastercard, Visa, Amex.
Accommodation: 2-bedroom luxury cottage (sleeps 6); min. 4- night lets weekdays,
min. 2 nights weekends; £80 per night.
Bitters: Greene King IPA, Marstons Pedigree, Wexford, 2 guests.
Lagers: Kronenbourg, Harp Extra.

Examples from lunch menu (Mon - Sat, trad. roasts on Sundays): *Chinese-style filo prawns; trio of croissants; salmon supreme; steaks; provencale pancake; spinach eclaire; omelettes; jacket potatoes; sandwiches; daily specials eg crab salad, mixed grill, chicken supreme with basil & pasta. White chocolate & Amaretto gateau; profiteroles & toffee sauce; raspberry mousse with shortbread; oranges & pineapple with rum caramel.*

Examples from evening menu (Tues - Sat): *prawn & mango parcels; grilled goats' cheese on crusty crouton; sea bass fillet with Noilly Prat sauce & grapes, finished with cream; whole grilled lobster; guinea fowl supreme; wild mushroom & asparagus puff; stilton soufflé; paella; fondue.*

The last man to be stocked in England suffered the indignity on the village green in front of this idyllic 17th-century thatched inn. At least he had something nice to look at: the mellow honeystone cottages are a delight on the eye. So, too, is the product of the kitchen of Tony and Sarah Martin, who over 12 years have made this one of the most popular and respected places to eat for miles around, rated highly by the national guides. Everything, including desserts, is freshly home-made; vegetarian and seafood dishes are specialities. The rotunda conservatory is a very pleasant place in which to enjoy it. Functions of all kinds well catered for; full programme of events and theme evenings. Darts and carpet bowls; petanque in beer garden. Ask about the Gourmet Club. Near River Nene, Elton Hall and Bressingham Garden Centre.

THE TRINITY FOOT
Huntingdon Road, Swavesey. Tel: (01954) 230315

Location: A14 (formerly A604) Eastbound, 7 miles west of Cambridge.
Credit cards: Visa, Mastercard.
Bitters: Flowers, Boddingtons, Whitbreads.
Lagers: Stella Artois, Heineken.

Examples of bar meals (lunchtime 7 days, every evening except Sunday): *fresh fish at most times; fresh lobster from tank; samphire in season; queen scallops mornay; oysters au gratin; tiger prawns in garlic butter; John Dory; guinea fowl in red wine sauce; grilled mackerel Portuguese style; monkfish with Pernod & cream; steaks; mixed grill; curry; omelettes; salads. Sherry trifle; meringues glace; banana split; peach melba. Seasonal daily specials eg samphire, lobster, crab.*

Seafood is much in evidence - the pub has its own adjacent fish shop, supplied from Lowestoft, Humberside and Loch Fyne. Also unusual, unique in fact, is the name Trinity Foot, after a pack of beagle hounds mastered by Colonel Whitbread, whose family's beer is on sale here. The hunters eschewed the usual fox as quarry, preferring hares, sportingly pursued on foot. 'Trinity' of course refers to the nearby university college. John and Brenda Mole will serve you delicious freshly prepared food in portions to satisfy the most ardent trencherman, with special evenings like French, Spanish or Portuguese to add a little zest. Well-behaved children are welcome in the eating area or unleashed onto the large, safe lawn, and there's also a conservatory. Despite its proximity to the A14, traffic is high up on an embankment and is not too intrusive. Large car park. Featured in national good pub guides.

THE QUEEN'S HEAD
Newmarket Road, Kirtling, nr Newmarket. Tel: (01638) 731737

Location: at crossroads to north east of village.
Credit cards: Mastercard, Visa, Amex, Switch, Delta.
Bitters: Greene King, Wexford.
Lagers: Carlsberg, Kronenbourg.

Examples of bar meals (lunch & evening daily except Sun. evenings): *Greenland prawns with yoghurt & almond dip; terrine of chicken breast, peppers & herbs; warm saladette of wild mushrooms & babycorns; watercress & horseradish soup; baked salmon fillet with herb & nut crust; baked fillet of cod with crayfish tail, spring onion & hot cheese topping; mignon of beef fillet with stilton cream sauce; Cumberland sausages in stout & rosemary with mash. English pears in port & honey; chocolate & rum mousse; rhubarb crumble; lemon cheesecake; treacle tart.* NB: pub closed Sunday evenings

Atmosphere is an elusive quality easily lost. But recent renovations have actually enhanced the rare charm of this cottagey pub, said to have been commissioned by Queen Elizabeth I after her incarceration in Kirtling Tower. One could light on the magnificent inglenook decked out in riding gear, sofas by the open log fire in another bar, roof tiles on the floor, but special mention must go to the lower bar, an intriguing room with its crazy crooked chimney, behind which is a private function room. Reopened by Gary and Diana Kingshott in October 1996, and managed by Gavin Howard, The Queen's Head has, like their other pub, The Beehive, Horringer (qv), quickly become very popular for fresh, home-made food and good selection of wines by the glass. Menus are chalked up daily, fresh fish being a speciality on Fridays and Saturdays. Children welcome; pleasant garden.

THE RED LION

214 The Street, Kirtling Green, nr Newmarket. Tel: (01638) 730162

Location: from Newmarket take Woodditton Road (opp. Heath Garage; turn left in Kirtling village towards Cheveley.
Credit cards: Mastercard, Visa, Amex.
Bitters: Greene King IPA, guest.
Lagers: Kronenbourg, Carlsberg.

Examples of bar meals: (lunch & evening daily except Mons): *tomato, onion & curry soup; seafood pancakes; steak & kidney pie; lamb steak in mint marinade; pork escalope in Cajun sauce; chilli; plaice; rib eye steak.*

Examples of restaurant meals (as above): *soused herrings in Madeira; smoked duck breast on salad of endive & orange; whole 1lb witch fish grilled simply with lemon butter; scallops of turkey with pepper & pistachio nuts, finished with cream; roasted guinea fowl with soy sauce, honeyed apricots & buttered leeks; steaks; grilled horse mushrooms with spinach & brie, with provencal crust. Cambridge burnt cream; lemon & ginger cheesecake; chocolate delice. Trad. Sun. roasts plus alternatives £10.90.*

That elusive quality of consistency is probably best ensured by a proprietor who is also chef. Paul Lange took over here in 1995 after years of international experience in top hotels, and has restored the fortunes of this delightful 17th-century inn. A leading national guide has already extended recognition, others are close behind. But this is no exclusively 'foodie' pub; there's a good mix of eating and drinking going on. Two very pleasant dining rooms also serve for functions, and children are welcome there or in the garden to the front. Barbecues are organised ad hoc, and most red letter days are celebrated. Newmarket is just a few minutes' drive, and B & B can be arranged nearby.

THE THREE HILLS
Bartlow, nr Linton. Tel: (01223) 891259

Location: one mile off A1307 Cambridge-Haverhill Road.
Credit cards: Visa, Mastercard.
  Bitters: Greene King, Wexford.
  Lagers: Kronenbourg.

Examples of bar/restaurant meals (lunch & evening daily except Mons): *ever-changing, always fresh from the day's market; vegetarian dishes a speciality. Trad. Sun. roasts.*

NB: closed all day Mondays except Bank Hols.

After a two-year sojourn overseas, Sue and Steve Dixon and family are back at the helm of this freehouse, which is good news for those who care that we still have some genuine pubs. Highly successful though they were (acknowledged by most leading national guides), they are not simply repeating the old ways. They declined to give examples from the menu simply because there is none; it's chalked daily on a blackboard, according to whatever has been a good buy on the day's markets. Unchanged, though, is their quintessentially English 15th-century inn: oak beams blend with polished brasswork and inglenooks, logs burning within when needed. The very pleasant walled garden also has a covered patio. It's all somewhat off the well trodden path, and juke boxes and the like do not blight the tranquility. The eponymous hills are Roman burial mounds, of great interest to antiquarians. Car parking.

THE EATON OAK

Crosshall Road, Eaton Ford, St Neots. Tel: (01480) 219555 Fax: (01480) 407520

Location: at junction of A1 with B645.
Credit cards: Mastercard, Visa, Eurocard, Amex.
Accommodation: 9 dbls/twins; all en-suite, phone, satellite TV, tea & coff.
Bitters: Charles Wells Eagle, Fargo & Bombardier.
Lagers: Red Stripe, McEwans.

Examples of bar meals (lunch & evening, 7 days): *chicken breast with stilton & bacon wrapped in puff pastry; steak au poivre; minted lamb steak; curry; chilli; lasagne; steak & kidney pie; Covent Garden pie; veg. tikka masala; oak-smoked haddock poached in milk & butter; ploughman's; sandwiches.*

Examples of restaurant meals (as above): *crispy coated brie in orange sauce; Japanese prawns; smoked seafood platter; steaks & grills; Cajun chicken; fresh fish; salmon en croute. Pear William shortcake; summer fruit pudding; apple strudel; raspberry meringue surprise. Trad. Sun. roasts. NB: Food available.*

NB: FOOD AVAILABLE ALL DAY SUNDAY

Charles Wells Brewery prefers its managed houses to be individual rather than formulaic; being family-run, this one is no exception. Value and quality are the watch-words; food is freshly prepared and chalked daily on a blackboard. This former 18th-century farmhouse has been refurbished in style: thick carpeting and upholstery, wood panelling, brick arches, quality prints. The conservatory restaurant (available for functions) is especially attractive, with its small elevated 'galleries'. The normal laid-back atmosphere gives way now and again to live jazz, quiz nights and special occasions such as New Year and Beaujolais Evening. Well appointed accommodation is in a separate block, is well placed for local attractions like Grafham Water, and is only one hour from London. Children welcome. Small patio to front.

NEW SUN INN & RESTAURANT
20 High Street, Kimbolton. Tel: (01480) 860052

Location: on main street, village centre.
Credit cards: Mastercard, Visa, Switch, Delta.
Bitters: Charles Wells, guest.
Lagers: Red Stripe, McEwans.

Examples of bar meals (lunch & evening, except Sun. & Mon. evenings): *steak & kidney pudding (speciality); pork & leek sausage; home-made picnic pie; chicken, asparagus & wine pie; chicken & mushroom lasagne; chilli; fresh fish dishes; mushroom stroganoff; jacket potatoes; doorstep sandwiches. Jam roly poly; bread, butter & brandy pudding; spotted dick; banana brulé; Belgian chocolate ice cream.*

Examples of restaurant meals (as above): *lobster thermidor; steaks; pork stroganoff; chicken stuffed with smoked salmon in white wine sauce; magret of duck; rack of lamb; vegetarian pasta of the day; daily specials eg Grafham fresh trout in pink peppercorn sauce; grouse sauted in wine. Hot chocolate fudge & walnut pudding (speciality). Trad. Sun. roasts.*

NB: OPEN ALL DAY SUNDAY

Kimbolton is one of the region's most striking and historic villages, dominated at one end by Kimbolton Castle, once home to Catherine of Aragon (she died there) but now a school (open to the public at certain weekends). King John initiated the 'Statute Fair' (known as 'Statty Fair') in the 13th century; it's still held in the main street on the third Wednesday of September, on condition that if it misses a year it can never be held again. But neither should one miss a visit to this unusual 16th-century hostelry, acquired a couple of years ago by Steve and Elaine Rogers. Despite the breadth of the menu, food is home-made, served in the modern conservatory or ancient restaurant. Look out for 'ram-roasts' on the patio, or theme nights, such as Italian. Children welcome. Easy parking on street.

YE OLDE PLOUGH
Bolnhurst, nr Bedford.Tel: (01234) 376274

Location: Bolnhurst Top End, to south of village.
Credit cards: Mastercard, Visa, Amex.
Bitters: Ruddles Best, Courage Directors, guest.
Lagers: McEwans, Fosters.

Examples of bar meals (lunch & evening, 7 days): *brie fritters with apple & ginger chutney; smoked fish paté; salmon & broccoli pancake with salad; Thai fresh prawn curry; Victorian kedgeree; fresh haddock & chips; steak & kidney pie with herb dumplings; steaks; lentil & spinach bake; aubergine, tomatoes & onions on bed of tagliatelle. Jamaican bananas; treacle tart; creme brulée; blueberry & marzipan pie; crushed meringues laced with brandy with raspberry coulis.*

'Unconventional' is a word that springs to mind. Landlady (since 1983) Rita is a faith healer (no charge!), and also holds yoga classes on the lawn (Weds 10am) in warm weather. Those seeking spiritual solace may book a Clairvoyant Evening (Mondays, 20 mins, £7.50), but it was during a 'Medium Evening' in the kitchen that contact was made with Cedric, 6'4" tall, pot-bellied and a former tennant. Barn and Country Dancing on the lawn (ticket only) are strictly for the living (leave your inhibitions at home!). But let us not forget that this is a first class pub, highly rated by the main national guides, with interesting, ever-changing menus and 18 wines by the glass. It's also a fabulous building to make overseas visitors gape, in a lovely setting with a pond and thousands of bulbs. Children welcome (and dogs) until 9pm. Darts, skittle and pool. Upstairs dining room.

THE BELL

Horsefair Lane, Odell. Tel: (01234) 720254

Location: village centre.
Credit cards: not accepted.
Bitters: Greene King.
Lagers: Carling, Kronenbourg, Stella Artois.

Examples of bar meals (lunch & evening, 7 days, except Sun. evenings in winter): *venison casserole; spicy chicken casserole; stilton, walnut & cream cheese pie; spinach, bacon & cream cheese roulade; creamy fish, mushroom & broccoli pie; shepherds pie; steak & kidney pie; turkey, leek & mushroom pie; chicken Kiev. Bakewell tart; boozy chocolate mousse; pecan nut pie; whisky ginger cream; pineapple raisin cheesecake.*

NB: open ALL DAY SAT. & SUN. in summer (food at normal hours).

It looks every inch the ideal thatched counry pub, and for once appearances are not deceiving. Tucked away in a quiet village not far from Odell Country Park, its 16th-century origins are apparent from the superb inglenook and exposed beams in the five rather cosy bar areas. One may eat anywhere (including the patio) and be sure of good, home-cooked food, prepared by the landlady herself, Doreen Scott. She and husband Derek have, over the past 12 years, earned the respect of the major national guides and local people, who appreciate the friendly atmosphere and absence of wailing jukeboxes etc. Children have an area set aside for them but will be sure to head for the little river which tumbles past the end of the garden (when not in drought!).

THE KING'S ARMS
London Road, Sandy Tel: (01767) 680276

Location: just off A1 near Wards of Sandy (easiest approached from north).
Credit cards: Mastercard, Visa, Switch, Amex.
Accommodation: 4 dbls/twins in chalets; all en-suite, TV, tea & coff;
£30 per chalet, brkfst extra.
Bitters: Greene King, Rayments.
Lagers: Harp, Kronenbourg, Stell Artois.

Examples of bar meals (lunch & evening except Sun. evening): *home-made paté; beef casserole; home-made pie of the day; curry; steak; scampi; plaice; salads; ploughman's; sandwiches; jacket potatoes; daily specials eg beef korma, venison pie, Whitby haddies. Home-made trifles; fruit salad; lemon lush; chocolate profiteroles.*

Examples of restaurant meals (as above): *fillet stilton (speciality); pork Somerset; beef stroganoff; game pie; grilled Dover sole; fillet of salmon in asparagus sauce; venison steak with cranberry sauce; spinach & ricotta cheese cannelloni. Trad. Sun. roasts.*

The many admirers (including major national guides) of Ken and Jean Parry during their 13 years at The Mad Dog, Little Odell, should note that they are now resident proprietors of this warm, characterful and refurbished 17th-century coaching inn on the old Gt North Road. As ever, they offer "sustenance and shelter" to the weary traveller, in the form of a wide range of chef-prepared food, good wines and ales, and very affordable accommodation, well suited to business people or visitors to RSPB, Old Warden Aerodrome and Swiss Gardens. A small function room takes up to 14 people. Children are welcome in the dining room up to 8pm; the garden has a barbecue (occasional) and four petanque courts.

THE HARE & HOUNDS
Old Warden, nr Bedford. Tel: (01767) 627225

Location: village high street, 5 mins from A1, west from Biggleswade,
15 mins from Bedford.
Credit cards: Mastercard, Visa, Switch, JCB.
Bitters: Adnams, Old Speckled Hen, Chas Wells Eagle, IPA, Bombardier.
Lagers: Red Stripe, McEwans, Bitburger, Kellerbrau.
Photo courtesy Dave Hillyard

Examples of bar meals (lunch & evening, 7 days; OPEN FOR FOOD EVERY DAY UP TO 11PM, but not always in the afternoon): *sesame prawn toasts with seafood dip; large French-style omelettes; steak & kidney pie; cod; scampi; steaks; lime & ginger chicken; rosemary & garlic lamb; deep shortcrust savoury vegetable flan; daily specials eg lamb sabzi, turkey korma, pasta dishes, rich cheesy pudding. Chocolate challenge; fruit crumbles; syrup sponge; super ice creams; light bread & butter pudding. Traditional Sunday roasts (choice of 2 with fresh steamed veg). Booking advised at all times.*

Here is a village to dispel any notion that Bedfordshire has nothing worth turning off the A1 for; a 'stage-set' vision of thatched 18th-century cottages clustered in a fold in the rolling countryside. It is also home to one of the county's better pubs, under family ownership since spring 1995. With many years' experience garnered in Berkshire, their philosophy is that this is not a restaurant selling beer, but a pub selling food. The latter is home-cooked, always using fresh ingredients, and served in platefuls, but drinkers are always welcome; no more than half the tables may be reserved and the atmosphere is very informal throughout the four bars, each with a charm of its own (one celebrates the life of aviator Richard Shuttleworth - the famous Shuttleworth Collection and Swiss Gardens are very nearby). Sheltered courtyard in the large garden. Family room usually available.

THE CHEQUERS
Queen Street, Stotfold. Tel: (01462) 730495

Location: east side of town; from by-pass, on to main street
(old A507), first right.
Credit cards: Mastercard, Visa, Diners, Amex.
Bitters: Greene King, Rayments, occasional guest.
Lagers: Harp, Kronenbourg, Stella Artois.

Examples of bar/restaurant meals (available ALL DAY & EVERY DAY): *home-made chicken liver paté; mozarella melt; large leg of roast lamb in mint sauce gravy; char-grilled steaks; pork fillet in cherry sauce; tournedos rossini; pan-fried cod in lemon butter; vegetarian selection; home-made pizzas (take away or delivery); fresh fish & chips (Fridays); sandwiches; baguettes; omelettes; ploughman's; daily specials eg home-made curries, steak & ale pie. Home-made passion by chocolate; lemon cheesequake; raspberry mould. Trad. Sun. roasts.*

Being open all day, every day, and just minutes' from the A1, this appealing 16th-century inn, tucked away in a residential street just off the main road, is a Godsend to the weary traveller, as well as an agreeable watering hole for those just seeking good, home-made food. Masterchef Douglas Bollen took over here with wife Paula in June 1996, and has effected a considerable transformation, and has recently completely refurbished throughout. The dining room (doubles for functions) is located in a new extension, beamed and chintzy, with old photos and other memorabilia of the area, but food is also served in the old bar, with a real log fire in the large inglenook in winter. Fortnightly theme nights include Jazz, Italian, Curry etc. Darts, pool and crib are indoor amusements, and the garden has petanque and children's play area. Duxford and Knebworth are nearby.

THE CROSS KEYS
High Street, Pulloxhill. Tel: (01525) 712442

Location: off A6 between Luton & Bedford.
Credit cards: Mastercard, Visa, Switch.
Bitters: Chas. Wells Eagle, Adnams Broadside, Old Speckled Hen.
Lagers: McEwans, Red Stripe, Kellerbrau.

Examples of bar/restaurant meals (lunch & evening, 7 days): *Cross Keys combo (spicy chicken, prawns & veg with dips); breast of chicken filled with lemon & tarragon; haddock royale (topped with cheese, prawns & mushroom sauce with breadcrumbs); steaks & grills; roast duckling; vegetarian lasagne; vegetable balti; salads; ploughman's; daily specials. Home-made fruit pies; wide choice of ice creams. Trad. Sun. roasts.*

When Peter and Sheila Meads took over a pint of bitter was 71/2d (old pence), soup was 1/6 and a steak 12/6! That was 27 years ago; today's prices still afford excellent value, a temptation to eat out more often. The 60 international wines listed (clarets a speciality) are also modestly priced, and there are occasional wine-tasting evenings with food to match. For the past 25 years Sunday nights have been set aside for live jazz. Many top artists have performed under the 15th-century timbers - it makes for an unforgetable evening. The attractive restaurant (available for weddings and other functions) overlooks 10 acres of grounds - room enough for a marquee, barbecue, cricket pitch, boules and caravan park! Three-course (+ coffee) senior citizens' lunch £4.50 Mon - Fri.

THE OLD FARM INN
Church Road, Church End, Totternhoe. Tel: (01582) 661294

Location: 100 yards from church (village is near Dunstable).
Credit cards: Mastercard, Visa, Switch, Delta.
Bitters: Fuller's range.
Lagers: Heineken, Carling.

Examples of bar meals (lunch & evening daily except Sun evenings): *home-made soup; filled rolls eg fillet steak & melted cheese, BLT; ploughman's.*

Examples of restaurant meals (as above): home-made pies (speciality); *chicken curry; salmon & sole roulade with broccoli coulis; fillet steak stroganoff; steaks; pan-fried chicken breast in red wine sauce; vegetable mornay. Chocolate torte; lemon torte; toffee ice cream gateau; peach & apricot crumble. Trad. Sun. roasts.*

Only five landlords/ladies have 'reigned' here since this 500-year-old inn was first licensed in 1860; one served from 1905 to 1967. Present incumbents Nigel and Penny Bradshaw don't expect to match that, but in two or three years they have certainly made their mark with their skills in the kitchen, and with personal, friendly service. The single bar is homely, with a huge fireplace in which are a table and chairs, newspapers thoughtfully provided. The richly carpeted restaurant to the rear also has a lovely fireplace and nice views over the large garden. Garden parties are held in summer, and a marquee is available for functions. Mrs Bradshaw's pies and sauces are much sought after, but for foreign interest look out for special evenings, like Scottish, French, Italian etc. Whipsnade and Woburn quite near.

THE RED LION
Church Road, Studham. Tel: (01582) 872530

Location: village centre, by the common.
Credit cards: Mastercard, Visa, Diners, Amex, Switch.
Bitters: Adnams, Greene King Abbot, John Smiths, Marstons Best & Pedigree.
Lagers: Fosters, Kronenbourg.

Examples of bar meals (lunch & evening, 7 days): *liver & bacon, chilli, lasagne, French sticks, jacket potatoes, ploughman's, sandwiches, daily specials eg home-made soups, beef & mushroom pie, quiche lorraine, salads, vegetable pasta bake. Apple pie; spotted dick.*

Examples of restaurant meals (as above): *Thai-style crab cakes; filo prawns with sweet & sour dip; avocado pear with raspberry vinaigrette. Haddock & sour cream gratin; stewed chicken with pineapple & ginger sauce; spicy cinammon lamb chops; chicken & avocado stroganoff; steaks; liver Normandy; mixed bean goulash. Lemon mousse cake; profiteroles with hot chocolate fudge sauce; bread & butter pudding. Trad. Sun. roasts.*

NB: OPEN ALL DAY SAT & SUN (food served)

Overlooking the village common and open fields beyond, The Red Lion is steeped in the best traditions of the country pub: warm and friendly; good, wholesome food and beer; time-honoured indoor pastimes; even a resident ghost (a candle is said to have lit itself one evening). But one welcome departure from the past is that unaccompanied women can feel completely at ease here. Others are monthly live jazz nights and alternative Theme Nights - national cuisines with appropriate music. Converted from two cottages (built early 1800s), the interior is very appealing, with leaded windows, dried flowers and attractive dining area. Children welcome - family room and garden. Whipsnade and Ash Ridge (stately home with lovely woodland) nearby.

THE GRAND JUNCTION ARMS
Bulbourne Road, Bulbourne, nr Tring. Tel & Fax: (01442) 890677

Location: by Grand Union Canal on B488, 2 miles north of Tring.
Credit cards: Mastercard, Visa, Diners, Delta, Switch.
Bitters: Greenalls, Adnams, guest; plus dark mild.
Lagers: Carling, Stella Artois.

Examples of bar meals (lunch & evening except Mon evenings): *Highland whisky fondue; Scrumpy Jack chicken; Irish whisky pork; drunken ribs; Bulbourne omelette; steak & kidney pie; bangers & mash; lock-keeper's lunch; 'canal loaf'; chilli; rarebit; potato boats; mushroom, pepper & coconut curry; fresh onion 'blossom' (deep-fried with blue cheese dip - speciality); blackboard specials eg cheese & mushroom bake, home-made vegetable pie. Boatman's tart; apple kebabs with toffee sauce; apricot frangipan; chocolate sponge with chocolate sauce. Trad. Sun. roasts. Afternoon teas. Breakfasts on request. NB: on Tues & Thurs evenings normal replaced by steak specials (from £4.95 for 8oz rump).*

"Innkeeper of the Year" (London & Home Counties) from the British Institute of Innkeeping is a recent prestigious accolade for Jackie and David Atkins. The garden of their 19th-century bargee's inn sweeps right down to the water's edge, and one can hire boats in summer - food and drink supplied! A small shop sells canal souvenirs. Other diversions are bar billiards, a shelf full of books, Sausage Nights (15 kinds), Quiz Night on Wednesdays, and every Sunday is Music Night - bring your own instrument (and there's no juke box or piped music!). Children will be amused by the budgies and a climbing frame. And naturally food is home-cooked and highly original.

THE VALIANT TROOPER

Trooper Road, Aldbury, nr Tring. Tel: (01442) 851203

Location: from Tring, turn right at crossroads by village pond.
Credit cards: Mastercard, Visa, Amex.
Bitters: Fuller's London Pride, Bass, John Smith; 2 guests
(1 special at £1.20 per pint).
Lagers: Becks, McEwans, Tennents, Kronenbourg.

Examples of bar meals (lunch & evening, except Sun. evenings): *jacket potatoes; open sandwiches; ploughman's; salads; many daily specials eg Cayman catfish, rabbit chasseur, lamb stew with dumplings, mixed grill, vegetable crumble, pies.*

Examples of restaurant meals (lunch & evening Tues - Fri, plus Sat. evenings & Sun. lunch): *French onion soup; stilton & apple tartlet; deep-fried brie in garlic; fresh fish of the day; seafood paella & kebabs; beef carbonnade; chicken annaise; steaks, sautéed kidneys moutards; tagliatelle quatro formaggio. Bakewell tart; creme brulée; fruit crumbles; banoffee pie; bread & butter pudding; chocolate fudge cake.*

Perhaps the most picturesque village in the Chilterns, Aldbury is also blessed with this fine 17th-century pub, under the same ownership for over 17 years. Reputedly Wellington met his troops here (hence the name); it is not recorded whether they had lunch, but it would make an excellent venue today. Food is of a high order, using fresh, local produce - the kitchen frequently runs out, so get there early! The military theme is celebrated by dozens of prints throughout the intriguing bars and dining room (available for functions), in which the original oak timbers remain untouched, and in winter wood still burns in the large fireplaces by which Wellington may well have stood. Children are welcome in the family room until 8pm, and there's a large garden with patio. Highly rated by most national guides.

THE BRICKLAYER'S ARMS
Hogpits Bottom, Flaunden. Tel: (01442) 833322

Location: 5 mins from Bovingdon (nr Hemel Hempstead); from the south, go thro' village, left at X-roads, right at next X-roads.
Credit cards: Mastercard, Visa, Delta, Switch, Amex, Diners.
Bitters: Marston's Pedigree, Brakspears, 5/6 guests.
Lagers: Boddington Gold, Stella Artois, Heineken.

Examples of bar/restaurant meals (lunch & evening, 7 days): *home-made chicken liver paté; seafood platter (noted); prawn & melon bake; Cajun red snapper; duck morello; steaks & grills; steak & kidney pudding; trawlerman's pie; huge combo; fajitas; local sausages; ploughman's; sandwiches; vegetarian dishes eg pineapple & vegetable gondola; blackboard specials eg thin strips of venison marinated in passion fruit & kiwi (served with rice rosti & kiwi coulis), artichoke bottoms filled with duxelle, prime Scotch fillet rolled in oats (pan-fried & finished with whisky sauce). Home-made bread & butter pudding; fruit crumbles; apricot & honeycombe bomb. Trad. Sun. roasts.*

Alpine by East Anglian standards, the Chilterns is a lovely area to explore, made very accessible by the M25. One of the joys of the peaceful leafy lanes is chancing upon a marvellous old country pub such as this, highly rated by major national guides for both food and beer. The menus are mouthwatering - staple pub favourites vie with the exotic (plus theme evenings, such as Chinese, Italian or round-the-world). Also uncommon is the service: orders are taken from table, not at the bar - licencees David and Sue Winteridge worked in hotels for years before coming here in April '96. The large garden has 100 seats; live jazz is performed there on three Sundays every August. Whipsnade and St Albans only 20 mins.

THE CRICKETERS
The Green, Sarratt. Tel: (01923) 263729

Location: on village green, 2 miles off jncn 18 of M25.
Credit cards: Mastercard, Visa, Amex.
Bitters: Courage, guest.
Lagers: Fosters, Kronenbourg.

Examples of bar/restaurant meals (lunch & evening, 7 days): *fish specials eg smoked haddock in creamy sauce, whole megrim with wine & grape sauce, prawn stir-fry, fish & chips; calf's liver with onion gravy; sausage & mash; duck in orange jus; smoked chicken & avocado salad; curry; chilli; lasagne; steak au poivre; vegetarian specials eg artichoke hearts with celeriac & potato rosti (with spring onion & white wine sauce); beef tomato mozzarella with fresh basil, mushroom & pepper stroganoff. Plum crumble; chocolate pudding; butterscotch cheesecake. Trad. Sun. roasts.* NB: open all day - some cold food always available; hot food all day Sat & Sun.

At the western extremity of the region, this lovely village is made very accessible by the M25. Yet it remains blissfully rural and unspoilt, just far enough away from the rumble of traffic, and with some fine country and riverside walks. Built around 350 years ago as three cottages, The Cricketers is now blessed with a roomy and stylish new restaurant extension; French doors lead to terrace and garden. With one or two necessary exceptions, ingredients are direct from the markets (Billingsgate, Smithfield) and prepared on the premises, including desserts. Seafood is a particular strength. Barbecues are held in summer, there are monthly quiz nights, darts and bar billiards. Children welcome. Facilities for disabled and baby-changing.

THE SUN INN

31 Lemsford Village Road, Lemsford, nr Welwyn Garden. Tel: (01707) 322247

Location: on main road, village centre.
Credit cards: Mastercard, Visa, Switch, Delta.
Bitters: Courage Best & Directors, Fullers London Pride, Marstons Pedigree.
Lagers: Fosters, Kronenbourg, McEwans, Holsten Export.

Examples of bar meals (lunch & evenings up to 8:30pm, 7 days): *home-made soups; curry; cannelloni bolognaise; seafood-filled croissant; deep-fried spinach & feta cheese goujons; potato skins with grilled mozzarella; burgers; jacket potatoes; ciabatta rolls; fresh-baked baguettes; ploughman's; speciality sandwiches (noted); many daily specials eg pie of the day, lamb & coriander curry, chicken lasagne, rib-eye steak, barbecue pork kebabs, Thai vegetable escalope. Tia Maria parfait; summer pudding; chocolate truffle cake; baked Alaska; apple pie. Trad. Sun. roasts.*

"The old mill by the stream, Nelly Dean" - this 17th-century pub was the inspiration for the famous old crooners' song. The stream still flows past, but the old mill is now THE place to be seen in the area. It gets very busy in summer - fortunately there's a large patio to the front - but there's always a good mix of clientele and the young bar staff cope amiably. Flagstone floors, exposed timbers and huge inglenook help to generate a special atmosphere, but it is undoubtedly the food which is the biggest draw (drinkers are always welcome). Anne-Marie (licensee with Peter since April '97) is a trained chef, and now again lays on special evenings, such as Spanish or French. "Noisy George" (deceased) is said to move barrels and throw pictures around -perhaps he objects to Karaoke Nights! Darts. Ample parking.

THE BROCKET ARMS

Ayot St Lawrence, nr Welwyn. Tel: (01438) 820250 Fax: (01438) 820068

Location: nr Shaw's Corner, 10 mins off A1 amd M1.
Credit cards: Mastercard, Visa, Amex, Switch, Delta.
Accommodation: 3 sngls, 4 dbls/twins (incl 4-posters): 3 of the dbls en-suite;
£45 - £70 per room incl.
Bitters: Greene King, Wadworth 6X, Theakston's Best, Morland's
Old Speckled Hen, 2 guests.
Lagers: Kronenbourg, Castlemaine.

Examples from lunch menu (daily): *home-made stilton & onion soup; pork & turkey pie; steak; speciality sausages; scampi; cod; salads; jacket potatoes; sandwiches; daily specials eg steak & kidney pie; game pie; shepherd's pie. Home-made sweets. Trad. Sun. roasts (plus buffet in summer).*

Examples from evening menu (daily, revised seasonally): *snacks as above; speciality steaks eg in red wine sauce with mango chutney & herbs; roast pheasant rossini; venison marinated in red wine with marmalade & herbs; roast duck; salmon cutlet with lobster & brandy sauce; pork fillet with creamy peach sauce; chicken breast with creamy Tia Maria sauce; daily specials.*

NB: cream teas served summer weekends.

Hurtling past on the M1/A1 it's easy to forget what treasures are secreted in the lovely rolling countryside. Lost amongst the undisturbed leafy country lanes, this picture-book 14th-century inn is a real discovery, but in truth is very well known and has been a regular for years in most leading national guides. Toby Wingfield-Digby, landlord since 1980, especially welcomes field sportsmen (and women!), and fresh local game is a speciality of the kitchen. The amiable ghost of a hanged priest is said to linger amongst the ancient beams - it was the monastic quarters for the local church. Children welcome - swings and slide in large walled garden. Small but good wine list, reasonably priced. No jukebox or piped music.

THE BELL MOTEL
High Street, Codicote. Tel: (01438) 820278 Fax: (01438) 821671

Location: on main road (B656), village centre.
Credit cards: Mastercard, Visa, Diners, Amex, Switch.
Accommodation: 25 dbls/twins, all en-suite, satellite TV, phone, hair dryer, trouser press, tea & coff; weekdays £49.50 sngl; £57.50 dbl; weekends £39.50 & £45 incl; Tourist Board 3 Crowns Commended.
Bitters: Flowers, Boddington, Boddington Gold, Boston, London Pride, guest.
Lagers: Heineken, Heineken Export, Stella Artois.

Examples of bar meals (lunch & evening, 7 days): *American burgers, sandwiches; jacket potatoes; ploughman's; many blackboard specials eg grilled skate wings, tandoori pork kebabs, barbecue sausage kebabs, poached smoked haddock, pan-fried lambs' liver. Japanese disc cake; ginger pudding; fresh fruit cheesecake.*

Examples of restaurant meals (lunch & evening except Sun evening): *creamed haddock & mushroom; seafood basket; ricotta Mexican; spicy chicken California; pork St Moritz (in apple & brandy sauce); char-grill steaks; duck breast cerise; fillet of lemon sole rolled with crabmeat with parsley sauce. Trad. Sun. roasts.*

In an area short on accommodation, these are luxury (bungalow-style) rooms at a budget price. Formerly two pubs, everything about The Bell is a little larger than life - the huge menu (all home-made using only fresh local produce bought in daily), international wine list, live bands on Sundays, and Cabaret Nights which attract top acts like Mike Reid and Jimmy Jones - known personally to proprietors (of 12 years) Tony and Gill Smith from a previous career. Good venue for weddings, conferences etc. Knebworth, Hatfield House and Whipsnade all nearby. Children welcome. Garden.

THE LYTTON ARMS
Park Lane, Old Knebworth. Tel: (01438) 812312 Fax: (01438) 815289

Location: mid-way between Knebworth and Codicote.
Credit cards: Mastercard, Visa, Diners, Amex.
Bitters: 13 real ales - Bass, Theakstons, Woodfordes Wherry, guests.
Lagers: Carling, Tennents, Warsteiner. Plus 50 Belgian bottled.

Examples of bar meals (lunch & evening, 7 days): *smoked fish platter; dim sum; jalapo's; steaks & grills; home-made steak & kidney (in ale) pie; lasagne; chilli; balti; speciality sausages (eg ostrich, Jacobite beef); plaice; scampi; cauliflower & broccoli with stilton sauce; jacket potatoes; ploughmans; sandwiches; daily specials eg spinach & ricotta canelloni, veg. lasagne, sweet & sour chicken, nasi goreng. Ginger pudding with lemon & ginger sauce; rich chocolate gateau; treacle & nut pie.*

Knebworth House is one of the grandest and most visited stately homes in the land, and this traditional 19th-century country pub is part of the Lytton family estate - old photos of house and family form part of the decor. The countryside in these parts is very pleasant - ideal for ramblers and cyclists - and after stretching the legs and filling the lungs there's good, wholesome food to look forward to, as well as an outstanding choice of beer (winning plaudits from CAMRA) and 50 malt whiskies. Over 2,000 real ales have been dispensed over the past nine years since Stephen Nye became landlord, with conspicuous consumption during the Real Ale Festivals every spring and autumn. Barbecues are held in the garden (with patio) in summer, which also has play facilities for children. Recommended by major national guides. No fruit machines etc. Large car park.

THE GREYHOUND

London Road, St Ipollits, nr Hitchin. Tel: (01462) 440989

Location: on B656, one mile south of Hitchin.
Credit cards: Mastercard, Visa, Delta, Switch, Euro, Electron.
Accommodation: 4 dbls/twins, all en-suite, TV, hair dryer, tea & coff; from £35 sngl,
£45 dbl incl; stay 2 nights at weekend and get free Sunday lunch.
Bitters: Adnams, guests.
Lagers: Stella Artois, Heineken.

Examples of bar meals (lunch & evening, 7 days): *liver & bacon casserole; chicken & leek pie; steak, ale & mushroom pie; bacon & onion pudding; cottage pie; pork in cream sauce with garlic & ginger; steaks; fresh mussels; jacket potatoes; Welsh rarebit; sandwiches; daily specials eg fresh grilled bass with garlic & black pepper; fresh plaice fillet with white wine & cream sauce, seafood pie, beef Madras. Louisiana lovebite; spotted dick; lemon brulée; toffee apple cheesecake; raspberry & apple yoghurt torte; speciality ice creams. Trad. Sun. roasts.*

"While you are here my home is your home." Landlord (since 1991) Roy Pearce and wife Wendy extend a warm, personal service which will never be matched by the ever growing (but, let us hope, temporary) infestation of ghastly modern 'theme pubs'. Built around 1900 (although the cellar is 300 years old), it must be said it is not the most outwardly prepossessing of country inns, but inside is agreeably unpretentious and comfortable. One amiable old lady (deceased) apparently doesn't want to leave (her photo can be seen on one wall of the small dining room). For a smallish establishment the menus are amazingly large and diverse, with fresh fish something of a forte. The well equipped bedrooms are exceptionally good value, especially with a free transfer to Luton Airport and discount car parking. Children welcome. Patio garden planned. Knebworth and Luton Hoo nearby.

THE PLUME OF FEATHERS
Upper Green, Tewin. Tel: (01438) 717265

Location: edge of village, towards Burnham Green.
Credit cards: Mastercard, Visa, Switch, Eurocard.
Bitters: Adnams, Bass, Courage, Flowers, Wadworth, guests.
Lagers: Stella Artois, Carling.

Examples of bar meals (lunch & evening, 7 days, revised daily): *4 or 5 fresh fish dishes eg tuna steaks, trout almondine; steak & kidney pie; sausage & bean pie; chicken, ham & leek pie; vegetarian lasagne/sweet & sour; chilli; curry; baguettes. Organic whole fruit ice creams & sorbets; bread & butter pudding; walnut & treacle tart; chocolate mousse.*

Examples of restaurant meals (as above, revised 6-weekly):*king prawns, scallops & monkfish tails in Pernod & cream sauce; whole shank of lamb coated in redcurrant, red wine & rosemary sauce; prime fillet steak wrapped in bacon filled with stilton; marlin steak on bed of sautéd leeks with shallot, dill & vermouth sauce. Trad. Sun. roasts.*

Now under the management of Tony and Carole Dawson (who successfully ran the Crown at Northhill for many years), this 16th-century alehouse (sister pub to The Bricklayers at Flaundon) is once again one of the area's most popular places to eat. Being in a very select neighbourhood, you may also find yourself rubbing shoulders with 'celebs'. There was none bigger than QE I, who used it as a hunting lodge. Period features have been restored with skill, but perhaps most unusual is the gallery, an opulent sitting room with Persian rug. The very attractive restaurant overlooks a two-acre garden (with sandpit, volleyball, boules and barbecue), which itself commandswonderful views over farmland - a great venue for a wedding reception (marquee available). Toilets for disabled; baby-changing facilities.

THE WHITE HORSE
Burnham Green, nr Welwyn. Tel: (01438) 798416

Location: on village green, one mile from Tewin.
Credit cards: Mastercard, Visa, Amex, Delta, Switch.
Bitters: Greene King IPA, Adnams, Burtons, Tetley, Caffreys, 2 guests.
Lagers: Lowenbrau, Carlsberg Pilsner & Export, Castlemaine, Carling Premier.

Examples from lunch menu (available every day, plus up to 8pm in bar): *filled jacket potatoes; sandwiches; fresh battered cod; local sausages; steaks; lasagnes; daily specials eg home-made pies, smoked haddock florentine, skate wing in black pepper butter, liver & bacon in rich onion gravy, pan-fried turkey escalope. Exceptional choice of home-made sweets eg chocolate, raspberry & hazelnut meringue; treacle & almond tart; fruit crumble; steamed sponge pudding. Trad. Sunday roasts.*

Examples from evening menu (daily): *coquilles St Jacques; moules mariniere; home-made patés & soups. Beef Wellington; salmon en croute; noisette of lamb with rosemary crust; blackboard specials.*

If you need reminding of what an agreeable county Hertfordshire can be, then a drive out to this idyllic 18th-century country pub is to be recommended. Warm and inviting, its timbered interior is on three levels, with a particularly attractive gallery upstairs. The dining area overlooks a large landscaped garden with duck pond, and there's also a heated patio area. Licencees Richard Blackett and Nicky Hill uphold high standards of cuisine coupled with friendly and efficient service. The restaurant has a no-smoking area, and well-behaved children are welcome at lunchtime and early evening.

THE GEORGE & DRAGON
High Street, Watton-at-Stone. Tel: (01920) 830285

Location: village centre, between Stevenage & Hertford.
Credit cards: Mastercard, Visa, Diners, Amex.
Bitters: Greene King, Wexford. Plus Guinness & Murphy's stout.
Lagers: Harp Irish, Kronenbourg, Stella Artois, Carling.

Examples of bar/restaurant meals (lunch & evening, except Sun. evening): *cocktail of melon, prawns & strips of smoked salmon on bed of mixed leaves with light lemon dressing; tomato & red onion tatlet with basil vinaigrette; fillet of pork medallions cooked with mushrooms, brandy & cider, served with caramelised apples; bouillabaise (selection of seafood poached in white wine, garlic & herbs, with powerful garlic & chilli sauces); millionaire's/billionaire's bun; fishcakes with yoghurt, cucumber & dill dip; pasta with spinach. mushrooms, garlic & smoked ham topped with parmesan; salads; sandwiches; chalkboard specials which nearly always include fresh fish. Home-made puddings.*

"The pub with the club atmosphere" is a fair description. Built as a pub in 1603, it exudes an air of comfort and well being, with its old beams, antique furniture and prints, and fresh flowers in abundance. To relax by the log fire with the papers (provided) and good food and drink is a simple but profound pleasure. But it is not only the warm hospitality which has secured a regular place - indeed a star rating - in the national guides; as a glance over the examples above will suggest, the cooking is of a high order and uncommonly original. Occasional special nights add further interest and the wine list is always excellent. Children welcome as far as facilities will allow, but there is a newly extended garden and patio. Ample parking.

THE TILBURY (INN OFF THE GREEN)
Watton Road, Datchworth. Tel: (01438) 812496

Location: village centre, at crossroads.
Credit cards: Mastercard, Visa, Diners, Amex, Switch, Delta.
Bitters: Five-hides (own brew), Bass, Caffreys, guests.
Lagers: Warsteiner, Tennents, Staropramen.

Examples of bar/dining room meals (lunch & evening Mon - Sat, plus ALL DAY SUNDAY): *oriental fish saté; home-made beef & ale pie; beef & venison pie; lasagne; chicken balti; prawn & veg, balti; chicken tobago; lamb rosemary; steaks & grills; salmon in mushroom & white wine sauce; fresh trout with prawns & garlic butter; battered cod; vegetable curry; vegetable chilli; nut roast; vegetarian sausage; potato shells; sandwiches; ploughman's. Home-made bread & butter pudding; fruit crumble; treacle roly poly. Trad. Sun. roasts.*

Ian and Sheila Miller's superb (and moderately priced) own-brew beer would be reason enough for a visit, but tee-totallers will also be rewarded by the home-cooking, on a menu chalked daily on blackboards, and vegetarians well looked after. On top of that, it's also a fine building, dating from the 16th century, with cosy alcoves and a magnificent fireplace in the dining room. The Ale Bar (with dartboard) is quite unique, having stripped wood floor, exposed brickwork and tables made from barrels. It is here that 'fun-ghost' Algenon manifested himself as a green haze, and he also likes to play tricks in the kitchen. Perhaps he likes the monthly music nights on Thursdays. Children are welcome and the garden has an aviary. Knebworth and Hatfield Houses nearby.

THE ROSE & CROWN

69 High Street, Ashwell, nr Baldock. Tel: (01462) 742420

Location: village centre.
Credit cards: Visa, Mastercard, Eurocard, Switch.
Bitters: Greene King.
Lagers: Harp, Kronenbourg.

Examples from lunch menu (not Mondays, except Bank Hols): *home-made lasagne; baked fillet of cod with prawns & cream; pasta Florentine; omelettes; baguettes, jacket potatoes; fresh fish & chip specials Tues & Thurs; daily specials eg boar & apple sausages, chilli. Ginger sponge with lemon sauce; summer pudding; chocolate pudding; treacle tart. Trad. Sun. roasts.*

Examples from evening menu (as above): *Toulouse sausages with fruit sauce; deep-fried potato skins with blue cheese; crispy prawn parcels with tomato & garlic; steak & onion pudding; chicken, ham & leek pudding; pigeon breast sautéd in rich fruit compote; pheasant supreme with duxelle stuffing; steaks; steamed sea bass with ginger & fresh lime; seafood au gratin; Tuscan bean garlic crostini.*

A regular in national good pub guides, this 15th-century coaching inn could nevertheless not be described as a 'foodie' pub. The menus are exceptionally tempting, but you are just as welcome if you are simply looking for a quiet, unhurried pint and good conversation in a convivial atmosphere. The bar is divided into four cosy areas, one set aside for games and another with a magnificent inglenook fireplace. But it is the 'nooky seat' which is seemingly most popular with courting couples. Children are welcome in eating areas and the very well kept garden to the rear of the car park. Ashwell is one of Hertfordshire's more picturesque villages.

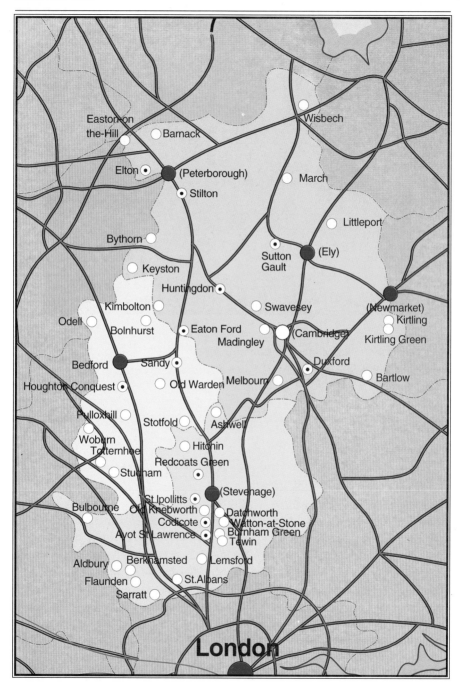

Easton-on-the-Hill
Barnack
Elton
(Peterborough)
Stilton
Wisbech
March
Littleport
Bythorn
Sutton Gault
(Ely)
Keyston
Huntingdon
(Newmarket)
Kirtling
Kimbolton
Swavesey
Kirtling Green
Odell
Bolnhurst
Eaton Ford
Madingley
(Cambridge)
Bedford
Sandy
Duxford
Bartlow
Houghton Conquest
Old Warden
Melbourn
Pulloxhill
Stotfold
Ashwell
Woburn
Totternhoe
Hitchin
Stucham
Redcoats Green
Bulbourne
St Ipollitts
(Stevenage)
Old Knebworth
Datchworth
Codicote
Watton-at-Stone
Ayot St Lawrence
Burnham Green
Tewin
Aldbury
Berkhamsted
Lemsford
Flaunden
St.Albans
Sarratt
London

● Accommodation

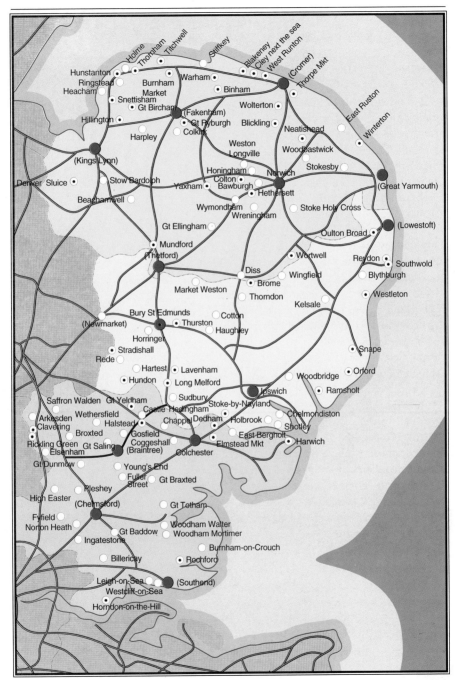

● Accommodation

*Accommodation

Essex

*Accommodation

e

*Accommodation

Suffolk

*Accommodation